Children of Imp
Fathers

Roger Shaw

HODDER AND STOUGHTON
LONDON   SYDNEY   AUCKLAND   TORONTO

ISBN 0 340 40849 9

First published 1987

Copyright © 1987 Roger Shaw

Typeset by Print Origination, Formby, Merseyside

Printed in Great Britain
for Hodder and Stoughton Education
a division of Hodder and Stoughton Ltd, Mill Road,
Dunton Green, Sevenoaks, Kent by
Richard Clay Ltd, Bungay, Suffolk

Contents

Acknowledgments

Much of the work described in this book was undertaken while the author held a Home Office funded fellowship at the University of Cambridge. Through this fellowship a senior practioner in the probation service is seconded to the Institute of Criminology for two years to teach and to engage in research. My thanks go to those staff at the Institute who helped and advised me.

The assistance and information I received from people, many of whom I had never met, must be indicative of the concern felt about this subject. My thanks go to the staff of children's homes, probation officers, social workers, prison chaplains and volunteer workers. I am especially grateful to those teachers and health visitors who corresponded, allowed me to interview them or completed questionnaires. My thanks also go to members of Leicester Prison Visits Centre Trust for their considerable help and support.

Whilst I would prefer not to name individuals, since so many did so much, I nevertheless must express my debt to Peter Francis, former Senior Probation Officer in Leicester Prison, without whose endeavours the samples could not have been taken, his staff, especially Margery Richardson, and Jane Maister the volunteer coordinator.

Finally my thanks go to those prisoners who agreed to be interviewed and the mothers outside who did likewise, some also allowing me to approach their children's teachers and health visitors. Because of these people and many others not mentioned, some at their specific request, some children in the future may, perhaps, suffer less.

The author and publishers wish to thank the following copyright holders who gave permission for their material to be reproduced in this book: B. Hounslow, A. Stephenson, J. Stewart and J. Crancher for the extract on p. 4 from *Children of Imprisoned Parents*; Pauline Williams for the extract on pp. 15–16 from *Criminal Justice*; Kate Phillips for the extract on p. 28 from *Nursing Mirror* and the Howard League for the extract on pp. 44–5 from *Unlawful Sex*.

Author's note: roughly equal numbers of girls and boys are affected by the imprisonment of their father. Rather than use the clumsy 'he/she' when referring to these children, I have used the masculine pronoun throughout. This usage is not to imply that the female children of imprisoned fathers are not included in our concerns.

Introduction

Every year in this country the fathers of thousands of children are sent to prison, for terms ranging from a few days to life. It is surprising that with such a large, and increasing number of children affected in this way, very little research has been made into the inpact imprisonment of a father has on his sons and daughters. The sparsity of interest shown in this subject is in marked contrast to the efforts being made on behalf of children of separated or divorcing parents. With the well-being of these children in mind, inquiries have been set up, research conducted and divorce experience courses mounted. Conciliation schemes are blossoming throughout the country. Books such as *Saturday Parent*, Peter Rowlands (1980), have been written for the benefit of parents who do not have day-to-day custody of their children. In the divorce courts the interests of the child are paramount and Court Welfare Officers (probation officers working in the divorce court) frequently describe access as 'the right of the child to maintain a relationship with the parent who does not have custody', as distinct from the right of the parent to see his or her child. In contrast with the increasing recognition of the plight of children whose families are broken by separation or divorce, children of imprisoned fathers have been ignored; seldom if ever do prison staff refer to a visit as 'the right of a child to maintain a relationship with the father' but rather as 'the right (or privilege) of an inmate to have a visit.'

Since the study of prisoners' families by Pauline Morris (1965), authors in different parts of the world have commented on the subject and almost two decades later Matthews (1983) again drew attention to the plight of prisoners' families in the NACRO publication *Forgotten Victims*. Despite this, there has been no examination of the impact of paternal imprisonment on the great number of children who experience it, and the effects, both harmful and beneficial, can only be surmised. Indeed there *can* be beneficial effects, as when a violent, aggressive man, or a selfish excessive spender, is shut away from his family. Jill Monger (1970) in her small but illuminating study demonstrated clearly the need for extensive work; that work has not been forthcoming. Why has there been so little research on this subject? Certainly the necessary information is not easy to acquire, but Davis (1983), writing in *Social Work Today* about a report of one of the few overseas studies which examined the children of imprisoned parents in a state in Australia, suggested there may be other, more sinister reasons. He commented, 'As the report says, public information about the children of prisoners is scarce. It further suggests that such a dearth of information is not accidental but "both convenient and necessary" because those who uphold the prevailing legal and penal ideology cannot afford to consider what happens to prisoners' children, as any recognition of their plight strikes at the very notions of "justice", "innocence" and "guilt" upon which this ideology is founded. As soon as the children of prisoners come into focus the major contradictions in the criminal system become glaringly obvious. When the legally-sanctioned punishment takes the form of incarceration the concept of individual punishment for individual law breaking collapses. Children become caught up in a web of punishment.'

It may well be the case that governments in some parts of the world would not welcome publicity of this nature but such an assessment is beyond the scope of this study. Suffice it to say that so far as the work described in this book is concerned no obstacles were placed in the way of the research by any official of central government, although bureaucracy at a lower level did rear its head occasionally.

This book is not only for probation officers, social workers and prison staff. It is intended for all those who have—or, because of their work and responsibilities, should have—a concern for children whose fathers are imprisoned. So great are the numbers of affected children that it would be unlikely that many experienced teachers, health visitors, school and community nurses—especially in inner city areas—have not encountered the problem. Whether they recognise it or consider it their responsibility is another matter altogether. Teachers and health professionals have contributed much to this research: to them much of this book is addressed.

Children of Imprisoned Fathers has also been written in the belief that the public at large should be and would wish to be better informed about this aspect of crime. Can one reasonably blame politicians for inaction when their constituents are silent on the subject? An effort has been made to present the material as briefly and concisely as possible, though there are extensive references for those who wish to consider some points in greater detail. For this reason there is a comparatively large number of footnotes, given the length of the text and a considerable bibliography.

The real test for a civilised and caring society, of our penal legislators and of the integrity of those who work in our criminal justice system will be measured by what happens now. To ignore this dark area would be to 'write off' every year tens of thousands of British children because of the sins of their fathers. Not so long ago we 'wrote off' illegitimate children because of the sins of their parents. How far have we come since then?

1
Hidden Victims

The Cinderella of penology

Although many years have elapsed since the publication of *Prisoners and their Families* by Pauline Morris,[1] little fresh information has been added to our knowledge on the specific subject of prisoners' children. This is despite the plethora of books and papers on the effects of imprisonment on a man's family emanating from Europe and the English-speaking world.[2] The few authors who have considered children have tended to support Morris's findings, despite the changes in attitudes and prison regimes which passing time has brought.[3] The fact that there is so little new information is surprising, considering the attention which has been paid to both civil and prisoners' rights over the past decade, and the awareness of other areas of concern about children involved in the criminal justice process. The importance of the emotional atmosphere in the home has been demonstrated in relation to delinquency.[4] Appreciation of the trauma of divorce and its impact on children of the family has led to conciliation schemes to help children and their parents through the processes of family breakdown or separation.[5]

The effect of bereavement on a family has been extensively studied, and support has been made available.[6] Machinery has been set up to try to prevent and detect child abuse and neglect; this currently occupies much of the time of health and social work professionals in many agencies. In this matter, circulars and directives from the Home Office and DHSS are issued from time to time.[7] Those inside and outside education who have sought to abolish corporal punishment in schools have been in full cry with pressure groups and literature.[8] Concern about child labour in the United Kingdom has given rise to a pamphlet from the Low Pay Unit.[9]

Bearing in mind these developments, the almost universal lack of attention to children whose fathers have been sent to prison is hard to explain. Certainly the relevant information is difficult to acquire; this may be why postgraduate students and academics have largely ignored it. The lack of governmental concern is more disquieting. This latter point will be explored in greater detail in Chapter 7. However, some research in Australia is of particular interest. *Children of Imprisoned Parents*[10] describes a study of prisoners' children which took place in New South Wales. It is one of the few pieces of work to be focused entirely on the children of adults in custody and to examine a sizeable number of cases. In the foreword to the report the authors write:

> It is with a sense of deep despair that we present this report. The despair comes from six months' of investigation in NSW Jails uncovering the desperate struggles of prisoner-parents to maintain viable relationships with their children. It comes from hundreds of hours listening to prisoners, their families and children as they speak of isolation, fear, anger and deprivation. It comes most of all from the realization that government departments and public policy seem hell bent on withholding the material resources and support that are vital to ensuring the rights of prisoners' children to adequate care and parenting.
>
> Government announcements in the last two months substantiate this pessimism. The freeze on public service positions means there will be no increase in the personnel necessary to provide support services. The possible cuts in foster allowances means there is little chance of extending assistance to relatives and friends of prisoners who are willing but financially unable to care for the dislocated children. The 'get tough' policy on prisons throws doubt on any hopes of humaniz-ing the prison environment so that all personal relationships are not destroyed in the process of doing time.
>
> Unless this report contributes to building support for a redirection in public policy, a redistribution of public resources and a change in departmental practices, the despair seems justified. Hundreds of children will continue to suffer—not because their parents are all inherently incapable of providing nurturance or support, but because they are systematically prevented from doing so.

It is interesting to note that these sentiments, although expressed some years ago and on the other side of the world, are relevant to Britain today—except that the number of children involved in the United Kingdom is far greater. It is a sobering thought that the UK government has no way of ascertaining through official channels how many children are affected by the imprisonment of their father, let alone what their needs are or how these needs should be met.[11] In a parliamentary answer of 27 July 1981, it was stated that 4000 one-parent families on supple-mentary benefit in Britain were headed by a prisoner's wife and that there were 9000 children in these families.[12] Taken at face value that statement would indicate that the number of affected children is not very great. However, one has to distinguish between the number of the prison population on any particular day and the number of actual receptions into prisons. These are very different statistics—a fact which has given rise to considerable distortion and misunderstanding when prison statistics have been interpreted. The actual number of children whose fathers are sent to prison in England and Wales would, on the basis of this study, appear to be more than one hundred thousand each year.[13] This is a vast figure by any standards. We should consider too that these children are predominatly from the lower socio-economic groups with poor support and are frequently from educationally disadvantaged families. The overall picture can therefore only be viewed as grave, not only for the individuals involved but also for the nation as a whole.[14]

Reference has already been made to divorce and bereavement. Changes in legislation and social attitudes have meant that in many quarters divorce is no longer seen as unacceptable, although it is only recently that schools have been encouraged to discuss it and allow children to talk about their experiences.[15] Workers on divorce experience courses which are partly intended to free children to talk about their situation, frequently report that it is the first time that some children have been given that permission and have felt able to discuss their feelings.[16]

The steady increase in the divorce rate has removed much of the stigma attached to the children of broken families. Imprisonment on the other hand involves a considerable degree of stigma.[17] It is possible that in due course the proliferation of laws, an increasing opportunity for crime, and penal policies which have led to an increase in the number of offenders sent to prison, may result in a reduction in the stigmatising effect of imprisonment by dint of it becoming 'normal' for a majority of males in poorer districts to have prison experience but whether this is desirable is another matter altogether.

The prevalence of criminal convictions in the population of England and Wales is very high.[18] Criminal convictions are not the sole preserve of a small minority of people who prey on the mass of law-abiding citizens. The range of children affected by their father's incarceration, although predominantly from the working classes, is increasing. Both the number of men received into prisons each year, and the total prison population on a given date, continue to rise; it seems reasonable to suggest that the number of children thus affected rises also.[19] The proportion of the male population who go to prison at some time in their lives is not known; when it is established it may well turn out to be surprisingly high. Similarly the number of children who experience their father being sent to prison at some stage during their childhood—say birth to sixteen—is also unknown but on the basis of the figures discussed in Chapter 6, half a million would appear to be the lowest likely number. It could be considerably greater.

Although most prisoners can be classified as belonging to the lower socio-economic groups they cannot be classified as being the most serious offenders. For instance, 25 per cent of all prison receptions in

England and Wales are fine defaulters and more than 50 per cent of men sentenced to prison are given six months or less.[20]

Recorded crime is mainly a working class, urban phenomenom with a tendency for it to be concentrated in the poorest areas. In these 'problem' areas there is also financial hardship, poor educational attainment, low employment skills and bad housing.[21] It would not be surprising, therefore, if the majority of prisoners' children reside in the decaying inner cities and in the poorer council estates. Parenting in areas of deprivation and a high crime rate is fraught with particular difficult-ies.[22] Schools with a catchment area containing a high proportion of delinquents have special problems, and insufficient of the right re-sources to pay adequate attention to the children of problem families.[23] Nevertheless, in most prisons men can be identified who do not come from low socio-economic groups; a number emanate from the middle classes. The children of these men tend to experience different problems—which are discussed in Chapters 4 and 5.

Occasionally groups of people who would not normally do so come into conflict with the law. The suffragettes are one example; conscien-tious objectors and pacifists another. Such people may display different characteristics to the rest of the prison population. One of the samples from the author's survey at Leicester Prison, to be examined later, included prisoners convicted of offences arising from the coal strike of 1984-5. So different were these men in so many respects that they 'warped' the figures and it was only after they were removed that the samples on which part of this work is based showed a high degree of similarity.[24]

A factor which should not be ignored in any consideration of prisoners' children is the question of inheritance. Although during the past few decades it has been fashionable to seek an explanation of all crime in sociological terms, work on twin and adoption studies has demonstrated the possibility of genetic factors in at least some types of criminality.[25] It is not within the scope of this study to comment on this. However, to pretend that the evidence pointing to a possible genetic link does not exist would seem to be as unreasonable as it would be to take no account of environmental and political influences on a child's behaviour before his father was imprisoned.

Children of imprisoned fathers form a large group of victims; victims of the crime perpetrated by their parent and victims of the system which dispenses justice. In contrast with some other groups of deprived, neglected and children 'at risk', the offspring of prisoners have received very little attention from researchers and as discussed in Chapter 7, still less from the agencies considered by the public to have some responsibil-ity for them. They are without doubt the Cinderella of penology—unrecognised, abused by the system and neglected by those with power and influence. It is because of this that *Children of Imprisoned Fathers* came to be written.

An attempt to rectify neglect

This study had a number of objectives: first, to gain some indication of the size and severity of the problem, in other words the number of children in England and Wales, who, in a single year, experience their father being sent to prison; second, to identify key issues in the parenting of children whose father is in custody; third, to investigate the attitudes and actions of agencies and individuals with a significant role in the child's life, such as teachers; fourth, the study was to consider the philosophical and criminal justice issues raised by the imprisonment of fathers. Lastly, it was to identify any major areas of need and make observations as to how these could best be met, bearing in mind currently available provision. These objectives have together one main aim, to draw attention to the subject and thereby stimulate interest, action and research into this area about which so little is known.

It should be borne in mind that the study was directed solely at the children of imprisoned fathers. Imprisoned mothers present different problems, some of a more acute nature but not within the scope of this research. Numerically far more children lose a father to prison than a mother.[26]

Research into the effects of a man's imprisonment on his children poses many ethical and methodological problems, for example the use of personal and confidential information held by social work agencies, counselling organisations and in medical records. What rights does a man in prison have in respect of giving his agreement for a researcher to speak with his child's teacher, doctor or health visitor? Should that decision be solely the prerogative of the child's mother? Suspicion of authority, which is common in some sub-cultures, and doubts about confidentiality, make some women reluctant to discuss their circumstances. How, if at all, can observed behavioural characteristics of a child whose father is sent to prison, be recognised as uninfluenced by the emotional atmosphere in the home before his conviction or the nature of his offence? A thorough look at the subject also requires the co-operation of many groups and individuals both inside and outside the criminal justice and penal systems, particularly schools. It also demands an adequate sample of men to be interviewed and to complete a questionnaire from inside prison if their attitudes towards their children are to be discovered and in order to gain some idea of the total number of children involved, since no official figures exist. Unfortunately, although the prison department has some information on the home circumstances of inmates, gleaned chiefly from reception interviews in prisons, this is not sufficiently reliable to be of use in the study of prisoners' children. There are a number of reasons. In many cases no outside report is available, and data obtained from reception interviews is based on what the man tells the prison officer without the officer having the opportunity (or the need) to substantiate it. This is particularly so in the case of short-term prisoners. Inmates may not wish to divulge the true situation at home for fear of information going to the DHSS which might affect social security benefit payments to their wife/cohabitee or to themselves after release. This is the case not only in instances where false claims have been made in the past and men are fearful of now being found out, but also because of a deep-rooted distrust of the system and a belief that it has a vested interest in paying the minimum. In other cases information is withheld because of, not to put too fine a point on it, the man's complex relationships. Whilst some men will boast of women that do not exist, others will be very wary of divulging any information about their womenfolk; the prison grapevine has many branches into the outside world and a woman whose man is inside may receive considerable attention.[27] The different rates of discharge grant lead some men to recognise the financial advantage of not telling the truth about their home situation; by saying that they will not be returning home to their family on release they render themselves technically homeless.[28]

The initial research

A number of methods were used in this research.

During two separate three-month periods in 1984, prison probation officers administered a questionnaire to men received into Leicester Prison who had been sentenced to six months or less.[29] The questions were chiefly about the prisoners' outside circumstances and family situation since this was the subject of the study.

In the period from April to June, 202 sentenced men (sample A) received into the prison agreed to be interviewed and complete a questionnaire. A further 26 declined, 12 fine defaulters were paid out, two men were transferred to other establishments before they could be interviewed and one was incoherent. During the three-month period from September to November, 246 sentenced men (sample B) received into the prison also agreed to be interviewed and complete a questionnaire. Another 15 declined to co-operate, 14 were transferred to another prison before they could be asked, and 13 fine defaulters were paid out. Another 24 men were omitted either because they were ill or incoherent, or on account of pressure of work in the prison probation department. Included in the 246 men constituting sample B were 33 known to have been sentenced for coal strike related offences, mostly occurring on picket lines. As explained earlier, these offenders displayed characteristics so different from those of the rest of the prison population that they have been removed from the sample and examined as a separate group.[24] Other sub-groups of inmates, namely fine defaulters, did not display significant differences from the rest of the sample. Additionally, a small sample of 47 men received into Bedford Prison during February, March and April 1985 was examined and found to have similar characteristics to the Leicester men.

Table 1 shows the marital status of men in the two samples, all of whom were over 21 because of the nature of Leicester Prison. It is apparent that more than half stated that they had no current cohabiting relationship with a woman.

Table 1 *Marital status of men at time of sentence*

Marital situation	Sample A n=202 %	Sample B n=213 %
Married, living with wife	22.2	28
Living with cohabitee	22.5	19.8
Married, not living with wife or cohabitee, or unmarried and not living with cohabitee	55.3	52.1

This fact markedly reduced the number with responsibility for children at the time of their prison sentences. Nevertheless, a considerable number of children were involved. Additionally, three men in the two samples were known to be single parents.

Men were asked to record the number of children living with their wives/cohabitees and for whom they had responsibility. If the number of such children exceeded four it was recorded as '5 or more'. The total number of children with prisoners' wives or cohabitees amounted to more than 177 in sample A, and more than 201 in sample B. The figures appear in Table 2.

Table 2 *Responsibility for children at time of prison sentence by men with wives or cohabitees*

Number of children	Sample A n=92 %	Sample B n=102 %
0	23.9	19.6
1	22.8	19.6
2	20.7	25.5
3	10.9	18.6
4	13.0	12.7
5 or more	8.7	3.9

The wives or cohabitees of six men in sample A and 18 men in sample B were said to be pregnant at the time of sentence. Five in sample A and one in sample B were unsure. There were no answers from 25 in sample A and 19 in sample B.

Interviews later with some of the wives or cohabitees disclosed that some thought to be pregnant were not, and some thought not to be, were. It is possible that pregnancy was sometimes claimed before the court case in the hope that it might lead to a lesser sentence. It is also possible that a woman may hide her suspected pregnancy from her husband at a time when his liberty is in some doubt. Either way, the establishment of early pregnancy in a woman whose man is likely to be imprisoned for an offence is a very inexact and problematic matter! The pregnancy factor should, therefore, be treated with caution.

In addition to children for whom the prisoners in both samples acknwledged responsibility, a further group of children appear in answer to the question 'Number of own children not living with wife/cohabitee.' In this instance, men were asked to record the number up to five, more than five being recorded as '6 or more'. The men in sample A indicated that they had fathered a further 109 children who were elsewhere following divorce, separation care proceedings, the result of previous periods of imprisonment or simply the man's lifestyle. Sample B acknowledged 101 such children.

Table 3   *Children fathered by prisoners but who were not living with the wife or cohabitee at the time of sentence*

Number of children	Sample A n=202 %	Sample B n=213 %
0	58.4	52.6
1	13.9	5.2
2	6.9	9.9
3	4.5	2.3
4	1.0	2.8
5	nil	0.5
6 or more	1.5	nil
no answer	13.9	26.8

The wives or cohabitees of men residing in the Greater Leicester area were visited in connection with investigation into the effects of the fathers' imprisonment on their children. This also allowed a proportion of the inmates' questionnaires to be compared with those completed by their womenfolk and for answers to be verified. Permission was sought from these women to approach the school, GP and Health Visitor, according to the age of the children. Where permission was granted the woman was asked to sign a letter to this effect for the professional concerned and confidentiality was guaranteed. A decision had previous-ly been taken to ask permission only from the mother since she was the person with day to day responsibility for the children.[30] The ages of men in the samples ranged from 21 (the lower limit for the prison concerned), to the middle sixties, with more than half under thirty.[31]

The catchment area of Leicester Prison consists of Leicestershire, Derbyshire and part of Staffordshire.[32]

Samples A and B combined produced 22 families resident in Leicester, where there were children for whom the prisoner had responsibility. These families accounted for 60 children.

Some limitations of this study should be borne in mind. It refers to one part of the country only and the sample is relatively small. It is possible that some men convicted of coal strike related offences were not recognised as such and therefore 'lost' in the total number of prison receptions but if this has happened the number would be very small. Also, the samples exclude men sentenced to more than six months. Bearing in mind these reservations, some interesting findings emerged and are discussed later.

Whilst this data was being collected, letters were sent to many social work journals inviting case studies and information, likewise to publications read by professionals whose work might involve them in some way with mothers whose husbands were in prison, for instance community nurses, probation officers. health visitors, ministers of religion, social workers and the staff of residential homes such as Dr Barnardo's. A considerable amount of correspondence was received including some from prisoners' wives unconnected with the Leicester or Bedford samples who had come to hear of the project from other sources. A letter was sent to prison chaplains of male adult and young prisoner establishments inviting observations based on their involvement with prisoners' families.[33]

The author has also drawn on his experience as a probation officer, as head of the probation team in a local prison for two and a half years and as chairman of Leicester Prison Visits Centre Trust for three years. This account is therefore both descriptive and empirical, considering the findings of the research along with the work of other authors, in the context of the criminal justice system.

Notes

1 Morris, P. (1965).
2 In addition to literature quoted elsewhere in this book, the following are of interest: Bakker *et al.* (1978), Brodsky (1975), de Crayencour (1976), Howard League (1979), Schneller (1978), Vercoe (1968), West Glamorgan Probation Service (1979), Wilson, G. (1984). Older considerations of the subject include Anderson (1966), Blackwell (1959), Fenton (1959).
3 Copley, C. (1981), Monger, M. and Pendleton, J. (1981) Wilmer (quoted by Monger and Pendleton op. cit.).

4 There is much literature on this subject but see particularly West, D.J. (1982).

5 See for example Francis *et al.* (1983) also Leicestershire Probation Service Divorce Experience Course Guide.

6 In this respect see Speck, P. (1985) and relevant literature quoted in the bibliography to his paper.

7 For an understanding of the issues involved in the prevention and treatment of child abuse and the great concern paid to this issue see Jones (1982) and the extensive bibliography to his book. Also DHSS and Home Office Circulars 'NAI to Children: The Police and Case Conferences' LASSL (76) 26 HC (76) 50 179/76 DHSS 'Child Abuse: Central Register Systems' LASSL (80)4, Home Office CI 45/1978.

8 Most of the literature campaigning against corporal punishment in schools has been produced by STOPP—Society of Teachers Opposed to Physical Punishment. The Children's Legal Centre campaigns against all physical chastisement of children.

9 MacLennan, *et al.* (1985).

10 Hounslow, *et al.* (1982).

11 In this the United Kingdom is not alone amongst nations. See Shaw, R.G. (1986) 'Kinderen van gedetineerden'.

12 Quoted in Matthews, J. (1983).

13 See Chapter 6.

14 A number of authors have commented upon the social and other characteristics of prisoners. See especially: Blackler (1968); Home Office (1978); Sparks, R.F.(1971).

15 Riley, Jeni and Lund, Mary (1984), Drake (1982).

16 For a comment on this see Francis, P. and Shaw, R.G. (1981).

17 See Page, Robert (1984) in relation to stigma as a fundamental and resilient component of social structure.

18 Farrington, D.P. (1981), Home Office (1985) Statistical Bulletin 7, 1985.

19 Prison Statistics show trends over the years.

20 Home Office (1985) *Prison Statistics England and Wales 1984.*

21 A number of authors have considered the part played by social class and occupation in the statistics of crime and delinquency. Most have demonstrated an association supporting the view that delinquency, whilst not restricted to the lower end of the class scale, is more frequently recorded in lower socio-economic groups. See Braithwaite (1981); Hirschi and Hindelang (1977); Ouston (1984); Wadsworth (1979); West (op.cit). Baldwin and Bottoms (1976) identified specific 'difficult' council estates. West and Farrington (1973) showed that within a disadvantaged inner city area, boys from poorer families were more inclined to become delinquent than those from relatively better off families. However, Riley and Shaw (1985) were unable to demonstrate a similar association but this may be explained by the nature of their sample, see the critique of their paper by Wilson (1985).

22 See Wilson, H. and Herbert, G.W. (1978), also Wilson, H. (1974), (1982), (1983).

23 See Chapter 5.

24 For a discussion about the differences between the miners and the rest of the prison receptions during the period of the coal strike see Shaw, R.G. (1986) 'Coal, Conviction and Calamity'.

25 There is considerable literature on this subject but see especially Forde, R.A. (1978), Mednick and Christiansen (1977) and the extensive references in the latter work.

26 Details of prisoners received under sentence, on remand and for non-payment of fines are shown in the Home Office (1985) Prison Statistics, op.cit. and are separated into male and female groups.

27 See Chapter 3.

28 The discharge grant for homeless men is £64.90 compared with £27.75 for those returning home on release. (Discharge grants are revised from time to time; these figures were correct at 1 January 1987.) Some prisoners in the study complained that the sentence was too short in that it did not entitle them to any discharge grant. However these men tended not to have children for whom they took responsibility.

29 A six-month sentence length was chosen for two reasons. It was possible to administer a questionnaire to all receptions in HMP Leicester if only short-sentenced prisoners were included because of the pressure of work on the prison probation department which undertook this. Also it is the short-sentence man whose family has been almost totally ignored in the past, who constitutes the bulk of prison receptions and who presents particular, unique problems in respect of his children. See Chapters 3 and 4.

30 It is appreciated that not everyone would agree with the matter being dealt with in this way. However, it has not given rise to any known disgruntlement on the part of the inmates concerned. Some men commented, when they were completing the questionnaire, that they were pleased to co-operate with the research if it might illuminate the plight of prisoners' children and lead to help for them and their mothers.

31 See also Shaw, R.G. (1986) 'The Prevalence of Children of Imprisoned Fathers' and Chapter 6.

32 The effect of this is that men sent into custody by courts in those counties go first to Leicester from where they may be transferred to other prisons. See Chapter 2.

33 22 replied, some at considerable length; this represents a response rate of about 25 per cent.

2

Prison and the Child

The system and its effects

The way in which the penal system operates gives power to the prison authorities to dictate where a prisoner is sent.[1] So far as males are concerned, convicted men are taken from the court to the local prison in whose catchment area that court is situated. They may then be moved to another establishment dependent upon their sentence length and the security classification which the prison authorities consider appropriate.[2] Very occasionally, what are termed 'welfare matters' may influence a man's destination but this is rare; length of sentence, security category, available space and institutional requirements invariably dictate where he goes.[3]

Prisons differ enormously in their regimes, structure and facilities; they also vary regarding visiting arrangements. The length and frequency of visits differ as does the ease or difficulty encountered by visitors in gaining access.[4] Some establishments have good facilities which enable families to come together in a reasonably civilised manner. In other prisons the environment is totally unsatisfactory and depressing, a situation brought about by lack of space, insufficient staff and the low priority afforded family contact by comparison with security, court productions and the smooth running of the establishment.

Thus it can be seen that the punitive effect of prison on the wrongdoer and on his family is not dictated or even influenced by the court, bears little relation to the offence and is brought about by an administrative procedure in which the needs of children have no place.

The minimum visit entitlement is a visit on reception, followed by a visit every month of no less than thirty minutes for convicted adult men; the unconvicted are entitled to a visit of fifteen minutes, daily, Mondays to Saturdays.[5] However, many establishments operate a 'privilege' visits system as well, and if space permits, allow longer time.[6]

The DHSS will pay for up to 13 visits a year for dependents on supplementary benefit but sometimes the journey is impossible for the family to make because of distance, location or health; also, the time allowed them in the prison may be minimal. In this respect the problems of remand prisoners and their families are particularly acute as the following submission to the House of Commons Home Affairs Committee on Remands in Custody illustrates:

The major problems identified are caused by the suddenness, uncertainty and unknown length of the remand. Unlike the majority of sentenced men (but in common with many imprisoned fine defaulters), the remand can be unexpected. There is frequently no solicitor or probation officer involved and information is often slow in reaching the family. One of the consequences of this is the inability of the wife to grasp the full significance of the situation and to deal effectively with the immediate repercussions. These can include a sudden absence of money because the man is not available to sign on as unemployed or due to ignorance of the Social Security system; explaining absences to employers in the hope that the job can be kept open and the various other material problems associated with all forms of imprisonment are not specific to remands.

Although the practical problems can be far-reaching, the emotional distress, particularly in relation to the children, is probably the most serious consequence of a remand in custody. The suddenness of the incarceration and the hope (however futile) that it will be of short duration, leads many mothers to deny the truth to their children. It then becomes increasingly difficult, with the passage of time, to be honest with them. The child may hear the truth from elsewhere and be unable to talk about it with his mother or father, and so turns to fantasy to explain the absence. This can lead to exaggerated fears as to the reason for father's absence.

Even when children are told the truth by their mothers and have an opportunity to discuss it, this does not necessarily resolve the difficulties. Remand prisoners are allowed visits every day but the statutory minimum of 15 minutes is all that is possible in many instances because of the large numbers of other visitors waiting. Visitors coming any distance, sometimes quite short distances, simply cannot afford frequent travel. The wives and children are thus reduced to the one visit a month financed by the department of Health and Social Security.

The effects of the remand in custody on the family can be far reaching and damaging; the unintentional consequences exceeding anything which the remanding court sought to achieve.[7]

Writing in the journal *Criminal Justice* following her visit to a remand centre, Pauline Williams observed:

The main door was opened and I had to fill in a form requesting the visit. The form had to be given to an officer who then sent another officer for the prisoner. I was sent to the waiting room. Down a brick lined corridor with high ceilings and bars over the skylights. The smell of disinfectant filled the air. I felt as if I had stepped back a hundred years just by walking through that door. I could not bear to sit in the waiting room, so many wives and children for their few minutes with their husbands and fathers. I stood in the bleak corridor waiting for my name to be called out. Finally I was led to the visiting hall. Once again a very bleak room with tables around three of the walls. The prisoners were seated on the inside of the 'U' shape and there were seats around the outside for the visitors. No privacy; next to us were a man and woman holding hands across the table and on the other side was a boy with his parents. The boy was trying to eat as many chocolates as he could before his short visit was over. After fifteen minutes an officer asked us to finish the visit. That was it; the prisoner was taken back to his cell.

What do you talk about when you know that you only have fifteen minutes? Everything seems so insignificant. Remand prisoners are allowed one visit a day but here the visits were so short. I drove for a total of four hours just for a fifteen minute visit.[8]

In reply, Wright, a prison officer and branch committee member of the POA pointed out:

It is correct; fifteen minute visits a day Monday to Saturday inclusive, if it were any longer you would not be able to fit, in a day, all the visits of say, some 200 to 300 remand prisoners. [9]

The prison system is a department of the Home Office and thus falls within the civil service. It is apparent, therefore, that the constraints relating to Crown Property, to secrecy and to Section Two of the Official Secrets Act, apply to prison staff. Because of the nature of the work in the prison service, which is essentially containment, security becomes a major consideration; the element of secrecy is amplified. Prisons are 'total institutions'; their nature exerts institutionalising effects on all those within their boundaries—staff and inmates alike.[10] Not only does the pressure to conform to the system affect uniformed staff and the governor grades, it also has the propensity to neutralise the civilian staff who bring professional expertise into the prison, for instance teachers, chaplains and doctors.[11] The pressure on prison staff is to do what they feel government and the public expect, namely to run a quiet, secure prison with a minimum of publicity or fuss.[12] This breeds a 'cowboy and Indian' syndrome wherein matters are seen in black and white with few if any shades of grey. Prison staff are on the side of good, the inmate is on the side of bad.[13] Prison staff get no thanks when a man is released and goes straight, no criticism if he reoffends, but there are far-reaching consequences when things go wrong in the prison itself. Take, for instance, the cases of Prosser, Hughes, Tuite and Blake, and the major disturbances which have occurred in the long-term establishments.[14] The result of this is that prison staff largely 'think within the walls',[15] believing that the outside world has no place in the running of a prison. The prisoner's child is seen as irrelevant to the management of the inmate unless it causes the prisoner to become a management problem. The low priority afforded family contact is apparent in the Prison Department document on prison design.[16] Unfortunately it would appear that in some cases the depersonalising and dehumanising effects of incarceration also render the child irrelevant to his father.

By contrast to the 'black and white' view held by many prison staff, prison probation officers see few aspects of criminal behaviour in these terms, but most in shades of grey. Therefore, probation officers working in prisons tend to be described by prison staff as 'softies', 'the welfare' and 'do-gooders'. The result is that when they intervene in matters necessitating additional contact between an inmate and his family they may be seen as acting on behalf of the inmate, gaining for him a 'privilege', when in reality it may be the well-being of the whole family or a child in that family that the prison probation officer has in mind.

Most prisons have a small team of probation officers providing specialist skills in much the same way as do teachers, chaplains and doctors. However, unlike these other civilian groups, who are within and directly responsible to the prison service, probation officers are seconded into the institution from the local probation area for a limited period.[17] As a result of this they are less vulnerable to being institutionalised, stripped of their professionalism, and their community based ethos.[18] They should therefore be in a position where they can constantly remind prison staff of the existence of a world outside and the importance of healthy family links. This is arguably the most important contribution which the probation service can make within prisons since it can directly influence the attitude of prison staff and have a significant effect on the inmate's family.[19] Prison probation officers are responsible for a social work service in prisons but there is no reason why they should have a monopoly of it. Indeed some of the barriers between themselves and prison staff can be broken down if uniformed staff are encouraged to engage in aspects of social work which experience has shown they are perfectly capable of undertaking.[20]

In order to provide an effective social work service in a prison, and particularly if this is to take account of the needs of the inmate's family, prison probation officers and any other staff engaged in the process need to have information about prisoners' home and family circumstances. Sometimes this is provided by the prisoner himself, by his wife, an outside probation officer, or perhaps another agency such as the social services. In the main, however, the most comprehensive social history is usually contained in the social inquiry report (SIR). The SIR is a report prepared by an outside probation officer to help and advise the sentencing court. This is a key document and usually the only account of a prisoner's life before he came to prison which is available to the prison authorities. Although prepared for the sentencing court, SIRs have wide distribution elsewhere and are used in prisons for a variety of purposes, much to the concern of many of their authors who view them as confidential documents.[21] Nevertheless, in spite of an expectation that people will not normally be sent to prison without the court considering an SIR, a great number of men find their way into custody without a report having been prepared. In only about a third of all the cases in the two Leicester and the Bedford samples was an SIR available to the prison probation officer when he conducted his first interview with the newly-arrived inmate, although reports were known to have been prepared in about 50 per cent of the cases. Delay in the SIR's journey from the court to the prison accounted for the fact that reports were not available in most instances.

There are various reasons why a report may not be prepared. Seldom will a probation officer compile one if the defendants is pleading 'not guilty', which means that most men remanded in custody will not have a report until after a finding of guilt or after a plea of guilty has been decided upon. Another very large group where a report will not be available is composed of men imprisoned for non-payment of fines, maintenance and rates. In the Leicester samples this totalled 36 per cent. Additionally some men are sentenced to imprisonment without the court calling for an SIR.[22] In some cases information gleaned during a post–sentence interview at the court by a probation officer may be sent to the prison and may indicate the immediate needs of the prisoner's family. This was infrequent in the Leicester samples, and in the absence of an SIR the prison probation officer usually had no information whatsoever about the inmate's family until he interviewed him on the day following his reception. In some prisons not all new receptions are interviewed because of pressure of numbers and the small size of the probation team, but in Leicester the expectation was that all new men would be seen. However, one of the findings of this research was that the problems voiced by the man in prison did not match those expressed by his wife. In many cases inmates made no mention of their children as a specific factor causing concern.[23]

The comments relating to SIRs should not be taken as a call for a greater number to be produced or for wider distribution. There is already considerable disquiet about the absence of confidentiality relating to these documents which sometimes deal with very personal and private matters.[24] It must, however, be recognised that in the absence of an SIR, those responsible for the welfare of a prisoner within an institution have no reliable information about his home circumstances and the needs of his family. In most cases the prison probation officer does not have adequate information about the prisoner's dependants and is ignorant of the needs of his children. So too are outside agencies, who may not even be aware of his imprisonment. This is commonly the case with fine defaulters, suddenly and sometimes unexpectedly picked up by the police and brought to the prison on the basis of a suspended committal warrant.

Such an incident is described in the next section.

The child as a recipient of prison discipline

A prison probation officer in a busy local prison received a note that one of the inmates wished to see him. Since this note was one of many, the inmate's request took its place amongst the others. It was six-thirty in the evening when the probation officer finally managed to see the man. The inmate told him that he had been picked up by the police on a warrant early that morning when he had gone shopping, leaving his five-year-old son sitting in front of the gas fire. There was no mother in this family; the father was the only parent. The inmate insisted that he had told the police officer that he had left his child alone but reported the officer as saying 'you should have thought about that before you defaulted on your fine'. (In subsequent conversation with the policeman, the officer maintained that the man had not mentioned the child, otherwise he would have taken the necessary action.) This meant that the probation officer was confronted by a situation in which a man had been parted from his son for ten hours and, so far as he knew, the boy was still at home on his own with the gas fire burning. Efforts to alert the duty social worker failed, since he was out on an emergency elsewhere. The probation officer therefore went to the man's home himself, the priority being to ensure the safety of the child, if indeed this was still possible. On arriving at the house it was discovered that the next-door neighbours, who knew the family well, had recognised that the man had not returned and had taken the child into their own home where he was playing happily with the neighbour's children.[25]

This incident ended without any physical harm coming to the child, but this was fortuitous. Other cases were reported of a similar nature where children were left alone following their fathers' apprehension or incarceration. In instances where the father is the sole parent, the repercussions of such an event are amplified.

Fine defaulters are only in prison for a short period, usually days, or a few weeks at the most, but the disruption which this can cause the family is out of all proportion to the length of sentence. This is especially the case when a mother, encouraged by the fact that her husband will soon be released, lies about his whereabouts to her child who subsequently discovers the truth from other sources.[26]

A person imprisoned for non-payment of a fine can be 'paid out' by the production by anyone of the required sum of money. In order to effect the release of a man in this way the money, in the form of cash, must be brought to the prison in which the man is being held. This can produce difficulties for poor families and those without their own transport. The man may be transferred from the local prison to another establishment such as an open prison or short-term unit, which could considerably increase the distance involved. The sum of money reduces for each day served in prison but the calculation is not sufficiently straightforward to allow most people to know how much is outstanding on any particular day.[27] Many cases have been encountered where the woman felt it her duty to raise the necessary cash in any way she could, and at whatever cost, to free her man, whilst he took a contrary view, believing the money could be better spent in other ways, or perhaps welcoming the temporary respite from responsibility and financial pressures. This readily produces family conflict, as does also the reverse situation when the man puts pressure on his wife to get him out, she having no resources to do so or else putting the children's needs first.[28]

Although the families of fine defaulters suffer as a result of sudden imprisonment and lack of information being available to the helping agencies, it is arguable that the families of men remanded in custody are in a worse position as the following case illustrates. It is an account of events that occurred in 1982. Names and certain details have been changed to provide anonymity.

In February 1982 Mr Newcombe was arrested, together with his brother, in a Midlands town, for alleged offences involving the theft of several thousands of pounds' worth of goods. The brothers were both self-employed and it was alleged by the police that they had been involved in wide-spread thefts throughout the Midlands and the south of England. The police claimed that witnesses might be intimidated and on these grounds bail was refused throughout the remand period which lasted for eleven months until December 1982.

Mr Newcombe lived with his wife and four children, aged twelve, eleven, eight and three years, in a town in the south. The initial impact on his family of his remand in custody, a novel experience for all of them, was one of shock, disbelief and outraged indignation, as none of his family believed him to be guilty of the offences. The first thoughts were to obtain his release on bail, and Mrs Newcombe went immediately to a local solicitor. Not having dealt with the legal profession before, and indeed ignorant of all matters to do with criminal proceedings, Mrs Newcombe sold the family car in order to raise £500, the sum demanded by the solicitor before he would take on the case. A subsequent application for legal aid, following information supplied by the prison probation department, did not lead to the recovery of the initial £500 given to the solicitor. The second priority facing Mrs Newcombe was to speak to her husband who was remanded in a Midlands prison some 200 miles away. Her initial attempts to talk to her husband on the telephone were prevented by prison rules which do not normally allow telephone conversations between prisoner and relative. (Subsequently the Senior Prison Officer in the remand wing of the prison did allow Mr Newcombe to talk with his children on the telephone while the call was monitored.) Mrs Newcombe and her sister-in-law decided to travel to the prison in the latter's car taking the six children of both families. Unfortunately, in the course of the journey, the car broke down and they arrived too late for the afternoon visits at the prison which terminate at 3.30 pm. Prison rules are not flexible enough in a crowded local prison to allow for unexpected mishaps such as this, and the two families were denied late entry into the prison. An overnight stay in a boarding house in a strange city, with six children, did little to alleviate the feelings of unreality, distress and growing panic felt by both women.

Over the next eleven months Mrs Newcombe made regular visits to the Supplementary Benefits section of the Department of Health and Social Security in her town to obtain travel warrants to visit her husband, and struggled the two hundred miles once, sometimes twice a month, bringing the children when she could, to see her husband. Previously accustomed to a regular and sizeable income from her husband's business, Mrs Newcombe now had to adjust her living standards to an income of supplementary benefit. Neither she nor her children had experienced such financial restrictions before, and her wish to supply her husband with cigarettes and food when she visited, meant that she had to go without other items.

The prison visits, when they occurred, were generally only of thirty minutes although sometimes prison staff were willing to extend this when the visits room was not too crowded and they knew the distance travelled by Mrs Newcombe. Unfortunately this was always an arbitrary decision and the couple had no prior knowledge of when the visit would be terminated. All conversations took place across a table with prison staff nearby. There were no provisions for children within the prison and the younger ones, after a lengthy train journey, tended to be tired and restless. No extra time allowance was provided for the children which meant that any conversation between Mr Newcombe and his children had to take place within the period allowed for his wife's visit. Endeavouring to divide his time equally between his wife and children proved a painful experience for Mr Newcombe. It was quickly apparent to both the Newcombes that whilst the prison tolerated children it did not recognise their individual rights to maintain a relationship with their father.

The strain of a number of bail applications being refused, Mr Newcombe's complete denial of the charges against him and his constant disbelief at what was happening to him, caused him to be agitated and impatient during visits. His wife's occasional failure to visit on a specified date because of sudden family problems, led him to worry excessively about her. In addition, the feelings of suspicion and mistrust that he began to develop towards the police occasionally spilt over into his relationship with his wife, sometimes leading him to doubt her loyalty. Mrs Newcombe, for her part, was upset at her husband's absence from the home and the impact this was having on the children. She rightly perceived that through no fault of her own, the burden of caring for her family had fallen completely to her. She had previously been very dependent on her husband's support and her emotional distress at his absence undermined her practical ability to cope. During the months of the remand first one son and then the second started to show signs of disturbance. The Newcombe case had received much publicity locally and the boys were subjected to taunts from their peers that they could not easily rebuff; they did not themselves understand the circumstances of their father's remand in custody. They had always enjoyed a close and supportive relationship with their father which had suddenly been denied to them. Mr Newcombe's attempts to explain his view of the situation to his children were severely restricted by the limitations on correspondence and visits imposed by the prison and by the distance from home. One boy became enuretic and the oldest son began to steal. Mrs Newcombe, feeling that she was partly to blame for not coping better, was initially unable to tell her husband of the problems regarding the children. She also did not wish to cause him any further distress, or reinforce his sense of helplessness, when she considered there was nothing he could do to remedy the situation apart from being released from the prison. He, sensing the problems but not knowing the details, felt frustrated and left out.

The problems slowly mounted; debts began to develop as Mrs Newcombe had delayed paying bills in the hope that her husband would soon be home to deal with them. Minor misunderstandings between the couple escalated into large-scale disputes because of their inability to communicate freely or regularly. By the time Mr Newcombe's case came to trial after eleven months in custody, his wife was on the verge of a complete breakdown, one of his sons had appeared before the Juvenile Court and his second son had been referred to the Schools Psychological Service. The telephone had been disconnected and the fuel supplies were in imminent danger of being withheld. Whatever the outcome of the trial, the damage to the family caused by Mr Newcombe's imprisonment, had already occurred.[29]

One of the most frequently encountered criticisms of the prison service voiced by prisoners' womenfolk was about the interpretation of rules. It would appear that it is not the rules themselves which give rise to so much grievance but the various interpretations of them by different members of prison staff. This is most pronounced in regard to visiting orders. Whether or not a woman who states she has lost her Visiting Order gains entry into a prison is said to depend more on her appearance and manner and the attitude of the officer on the gate, than on strict interpretation of the regulations. To the officer on duty a woman and her child turned away may be one minor chore in a long day's work but to the woman, who may have travelled a great distance, and particularly to the child seeing father for the first time for three or four weeks, it is an event creating anger and depression with consequent strife between mother and child. This is despite Prison Standing Order 5, which states that 'It is one of the roles of the Prison Service to ensure that the socially harmful effects of an inmate's removal from normal life are so far as possible minimised and that his contacts with the outside world are maintained. Outside contacts are therefore encouraged especially between an inmate and his family and friends'.

Judgemental attitudes which have repercussions on the children of prisoners are not confined to visits and letters. They also influence other aspects of the system such as home leave. In one prison it was apparent to staff that whether a man was granted home leave was dependent mainly upon which Assistant Governor chaired the Home Leave Board. However, the man's family would not likely know of this. In 1984 the Control Review Committee said in its report, 'Home leave is, in fact, a matter on which the practices in this country are markedly more cautious than in the rest of Europe'.[30] This rather limp sentiment is in marked contrast to the rest of the report which grasps some difficult nettles in relation to the grave problems which the long-term prisoner poses for the Prison Service today. It is another example of the low priority given to prisoners' children in the consciousness of those responsible for the prison system at all levels.

It must be borne in mind that prison staff are in a particularly difficult position. The fact that they hold men, most of whom would rather be elsewhere, makes the system the common enemy of the inmate and his family. The slightest discrepancy or apparent unfairness on the part of any member of staff is therefore magnified, sometimes out of all proportion. Notwithstanding this however, the varied interpretation of rules is a cause for concern and some reported incidents of women with children being turned away at the gate for a most trivial reason were seen by the recipient as spiteful.[31]

Problems associated with visits do not end once the family gains access. In common with members of the armed forces and the Merchant Navy, prisoners tend to read letters over and over again, particularly those from loved ones outside. Pieces in a letter are sometimes discussed with a cell-mate.

In the incident about to be described, a woman who had written to her husband regularly over a long period was finding it increasingly difficult to think of something to say. Inadvisedly in a letter she said, 'felt so fed-up and bored and lonely last night that I went out to the pub for a drink. Think it did me good, felt a bit better afterwards'. The man turned this **statement over in his mind as he read and re-read the letter. 'What do** you think about this?' he said to his cell-mate. 'Don't like the sound of it', said the other prisoner sagely. 'Guess it's her way of telling you some other bloke is screwing her. Happened to my last wife when I was doing my last stretch a few years ago. I got a letter just like that, it's a sort of "Dear John" in disguise'.[32] This, of course, gave the man more cause for thought and in the long hours of inactivity in prison the matter grew in significance.

The day of the visit arrived; wife and children came to the gate and were duly sent to the visiting room. After the usual preliminaries—a little talk about inconsequential things like the weather, a new toy one of the children was playing with—the man suddenly burst out:

'Who were you with down at the pub then?'

'Nobody! Went down on my own'.

'Don't give me that, you must think I'm green'.

The two children looked from one parent to the other as the argument became more heated, the accusations more hurtful, the denials more intense. Before anything could be resolved a prison officer came over. 'Sorry dear, time's up, have to go now,' he said. The woman watched, close to tears, as her husband was led away, tight-lipped. She left the prison unhappy, frustrated and irritable, snapping at every minor misdemeanor of the children and every word they uttered, as they went on their way to catch the train home. Both she and her husband would have to wait a month before the next visit, a month in which to prepare themselves for the next encounter. The children would have what would seem to them much longer; a month in which to turn over in their minds the uncertainty, disappointment and confusion generated by the last visit.[33]

Simply making the journey to a prison can present difficulties to a mother with very young children, even when a bus service is organised for prisoners' families, as the following letter from a prisoner's wife demonstrates:

My common-law husband is in prison which is quite a way from home; also there is only one bus which runs on every first Sunday. Also you are very lucky if you can get a place on the bus, so you have to book early and there is the problem of getting the visiting order on time so you can go on the bus. It is also inconvenient to me as I have one child of twenty months and one of three weeks which I am feeding myself by breast. Not only is there the problem of toilet facilities but children will not sit still for a three to four hour journey. There is the smell of messy nappies which have to be changed and may cause embarrassment. I also find it difficult to feed the young baby as it will cause embarrassment to others as well as myself. Social security do not issue train passes now as there is the free bus service but there is the problem of travel sickness with myself and the children so the long journey on the bus does not help.[34]

Although some parents do not allow their children to visit a prison, others do. Once inside, children can become a distraction to other families and a nuisance to staff as they react to the environment; others are quite at home. A prison chaplain observed:

Sometimes fathers refuse to allow their children to visit them because of a desire to protect them from the disgrace and horror of prison. They find this rejection difficult to understand and handle.[35]

There are children who are brought up in areas or families where criminality is a part of everyday living. Someone is in prison from many of their friends' family, so visiting prison is a natural thing for them to do. They look quite settled in the visits room, while the younger ones are happy to play in the designated play area. Some fathers with a long history of criminality will often lecture their children on the wrongness of criminal behaviour, but as their words are not reinforced by their actions, an understandable tension is created in the child which could lead to difficulties later.[35]

However, another chaplain wrote:

'I have some experience of observing children on visits. They are occasionally withdrawn but much more often they are ill-behaved, exhibitionist and aggressive.'[35]

It is evident that the prisoner's child is very low on the list of priorities in the prison system. Many of the barriers placed between the child and his father are unintentional or unnecessary. With willingness on the part of the prison authorities and the POA the punishment inflicted on the child for his father's offences could be lessened.[36] This possibility will be examined in Chapters 7 and 8.

Notes

1 The location, size and some other details of Prison Department Establishments can be found in Home Office (1984) *Report on the Work of the Prison Department 1983* (published each year). See also Prison Department (1983) *The Prison Rules 1964* (as amended).
2 For an official account of this process see HM Chief Inspector of Prisons' report *Prison Categorisation Procedures*.
3 Some interesting elements do sometimes influence this process and at times a man's family situation can be viewed negatively, for instance knowledge that an offender is worried about his family may lead to his being sent to a closed prison instead of an open establishment lest he absconds. See Shaw, R. (1981) *Who Uses Social Inquiry Reports?*.
4 Williams (1968), (1978); Monger and Pendleton (1977); Matthews (1983).
5 There are some exceptions to this. Visitors to prisoners classified as Category A for security reasons, may not visit until they have been cleared

by the police. Although usually this is undertaken swiftly there are occasions when it can be a very long process. The reasons for a delay are not always clear nor associated with terrorism risks. A prison chaplain observed, 'Fathers of adult children who have started courting face enormous difficulty in that the boyfriend or girlfriend can only visit after a security checkout which one hopes the police undertake with a great deal of discretion.' The governor has the right under Prison Rules to defer a visit if an inmate is confined to his cell for disciplinary reasons.

6 See, for example, HM Chief Inspector of Prison's Report on Parkhurst which operates two visits a month for up to three hours' duration. This was considered by the Inspector to be 'a sensible arrangement' in view of the location of the prison on the Isle of Wight.

7 Part of submission on behalf of Leicester Prison Visits Centre Trust to the House of Commons Home Affairs Committee on Remands in Custody (1984).

8 Williams, P. (1984).

9 Wright, J.F. (1984).

10 See Goffman, E. (1961) for the classic discussion of institutionalisation.

11 For a description of this process see Mathiesen, T. (1966) also Priestley, P. (1980).

12 This is discussed in greater depth by Shaw, R. (1982) 'Myths of Prison Overcrowding'.

13 See NASPO (1982).

14 Prosser was apparently beaten to death in a prison hospital. The case received considerable publicity; three prison officers were tried and acquitted and no one has since been convicted of the killing.

Hughes escaped from a vehicle whilst in prison custody by stabbing two officers with a knife he had taken from the prison kitchen. This incident lead to a review of reception procedures and arrangements for conducting prisoners to courts.

Tuite, an IRA man on remand, escaped, apparently as a result of other prisoners breaking through the wall. The matter resulted in a number of staff being made subject to disciplinary proceedings.

Blake, a traitor, escaped, following which a major review of security took place.

Riots in some of the high security prisons have brought criticism of staff and the system in their wake and a major dispute between the POA and the prison department.

These incidents are quoted as examples of the far-reaching ramifications of incidents within prisons; there have been others and even those given above had more repercussions than space here allows to describe.

15 See NASPO op. cit.

16 Prison Department (1984) *Current Recommended Standards for the Design of New Prison Establishments,* see also Casale, S.(1984) *Minimum Standards for Prison Establishments.*

17 The period of secondment is usually for a minimum of two years and on average three or four years.

18 NASPO op. cit.; See also Marsh *et al.* (1985) for a consideration of staff attitudes in the Prison Service.

19 This point is touched on in more detail in Chapters 7 and 8.

20 Shaw, R. (1984) 'Shared Social Work in a Local Prison: A Matter of Trust'.
21 National Association of Probation Officers (NAPO) (1981) Social Inquiry Reports—A Policy Paper also Shaw, R. (1981) op. cit.
22 See for example Willcox, P. (1981), (1983).
23 See Chapter 3.
24 Shaw, R. (1981) op. cit.
25 Actual case example.
26 This is a frequent occurrence, see Chapter 4.
27 For greater insight into the problems of fine default see NACRO (1981) 'Fine Default' Report of a NACRO Working Party.
28 See Chapters 3 and 7.
29 Knight, C. (1984) Leicester Prison Visits Centre Trust.
30 'Report of the Control Review Committee' (1984).
31 See Chapter 7.
32 A 'Dear John' letter is one which a man receives from a woman outside telling him their marriage or relationship is over.
33 Actual case example of a frequently occurring problem.
34 Letter from prisoner's wife sent at instigation of a Health Visitor in the north of England.
35 Personal correspondence from Prison Chaplains.
36 The Prison Officers Association (POA) is a powerful body. In many prisons it has a significant influence on the running of the institution and therefore, indirectly, on the children of inmates.

3

The Family Under Sentence

Economic consequences

The economic consequences of a man's imprisonment on his family can be considerable. They have recently been reviewed by Jill Matthews[1] so will not be repeated here except to observe that when a man is imprisoned for any length of time his dependants take on many of the characteristics of a single-parent family. In this respect the observations of Phillips (1985) are very pertinent:

> Many single parents are, of necessity, extremely isolated, to the detriment of their mental health and social well-being.
>
> Poverty is a killer. The perinatal mortality rate is twice as high among the unskilled as for babies of professional couples. Poverty permeates every aspect of single-parent family life.
>
> Half of all homeless families have one parent, and half of all one-parent families live on, or below the breadline (supplementary benefit level), compared with six per cent of married couples with children. The one-parent family is more likely to live in a condition of massive deprivation, with overcrowding, damp and decay, in 'bad' areas which many of us would be frightened to visit.
>
> There are more than three million unemployed people in Britain. Single parents are over-represented in this figure because society militates against them even seeking employment, simply by failing to supply adequate day and nursery care facilities. The State and employers are equally guilty in refusing to discharge this responsibility ... research suggests that the under-fives are more seriously disturbed than older children by divorce, and that remarriage can produce negative effects. A major American study shows with astonishing repetition how deeply children long for their parents to be reunited, and this longing persists.[2]

It has already been observed that prisoners' children come largely from the more disadvantaged sections of society. This was further demonstrated by their dependence on social security benefit. The two Leicester samples combined totalled 448 men of whom 22 were known to have 60 dependent children residing in Leicester city with a further two about to be born. Eighteen of these families were on social security prior to the man being sent to prison. Only one was known not to be, with three not known.

Replies from some of the Leicester women, and reports from correspondents indicated that although some families fared better when the man was absent, either because he drank or otherwise abused the budget, or simply because the wife was a better manager, for the majority the situation deteriorated. Sometimes the woman would be a less able manager, unused to dealing with the DHSS or taking on the entire demands of the household wherein finances were already under strain with outstanding bills and demands. It was evident from interviews with men in prison, especially those sent there for non-payment of fines, that prison can in some cases represent a temporary haven from the problems of the ouside world. The effect of this, however, is only to heighten the difficulties piled on the woman outside and thus on the children. Many instances have been encountered where a woman whose husband was imprisoned for fine default begged, borrowed, and in a few cases stole money in order to buy out her man.[3] The long-term effects on someone on social security or a very low income, of having to pay back what may be a considerable sum of money can be serious, and may store up further problems for the future. Not infrequently, however, the couple come to a decision that the little cash they have would be better spent on other things, such as the children at Christmas, than on a fine; prison is accepted as the inevitable consequence. In his speech to the Prison Reform Trust on 10 April 1986 the Home Secretary stated: 'Custody needs to be available as a last resort in default of payment. But prison is for those who will not pay, not for those who cannot, and fines must be pitched at levels which will have regard to offenders' means . . . '.[4] Would that it were so simple to separate those who 'can't pay' from those who 'won't pay'!

Although the less intelligent and poorly educated women have greater potential difficulties to face when the man is imprisoned, many rise to the occasion and cope well despite almost overwhelming odds. A health visitor wrote of one of her cases:

> One family I would call copers—father alcoholic, intelligent, unskilled labourer. He clearly knows the system well being a recidivist, and his common-law second wife is adept at managing the system. This family, despite having a child under five and two older boys (and various other children in long-term care) had had the electricity disconnected and no gas in the house. Father was imprisoned for about eight weeks of a three month sentence for assaulting a policeman while drunk. He has a terrible reputation with the police and I

am sure was in part provoked. The common-law wife managed very well, the community in which they lived was highly supportive. Electric current provided from back loo next door, battery TV, wood collection and coal 'obtained' from a yard. The father on release obtained a TOPS course in bricklaying in another town. I helped the family get a removal grant, they had already got a council house of their own accord. The dad likes prison because he cannot drink there. Altogether an extremely resourceful family. The children appear unaffected by these absences, they are rather dirty and under-stimulated but are optimistic about going to a new town and home.[5]

In contrast, some other women are so smitten by despair, grief and a sense of hopelessness that they collapse under the strain and are unable to communicate with their children. Very few are offered the advice and support they so obviously need. Those whose men fall within the responsibility of the probation service may well receive considerable help and referral to other agencies where appropriate, but most are not in contact with probation and frequently have no other agency to which they can turn unless there is a voluntary body in the area which is concerned with prisoners' families.[6] Such organisations are multiplying but the services available nationally are still most inadequate given the size of the problem.[7]

The problems of the mother

In addition to specific matters discussed elsewhere in this chapter, women may be subject to particular strains which in turn impinge on their children. One of the most commonly encountered reactions was an expression of loneliness and insecurity. Sometimes this was resolved by the aquisition of a substitute partner, but where it was not, the woman might become prey to unwelcome attention from men seeking company, sex, accommodation or a combination of any or all of these. Some women found this to reach almost intolerable limits. One prisoner's wife wrote:

I have been socially harrassed by old friends and neighbours as well as people spraying obscene words on my door such as slag, con, thief and many more. Also windows being broken and people sneaking around on a night frightening me and my eldest half to death. There is then the problem I get called names in the street by adults as well as by children. I can't even go into the garden because of these people and I dare not leave the house in fear of it being ransacked or similar.[8]

In interview another explained her feelings:

I've never seen most of these blokes before but they come round and try chatting me up like they've known me for years. Sometimes a bloke will be waiting when I get back from collecting the kids from school. The neighbours think I'm on the game. What with my fellow being sent down and then these blokes hanging around, some of them won't even speak to me now. It was the last straw when the social sent some snoop round because someone had told them that a bloke was living with me. I spoke to the council about being rehoused to somewhere else where people wouldn't know but they weren't interested. You've no idea what it's like, I never thought it would be like this. It's alright for him in there [prison] I'm the one that's doing the bird and getting all the aggro. Last night I felt so screwed up that I did something I never thought I'd do—I picked up the baby and shook the little bleeder so hard that its head nearly dropped off because it wouldn't stop its screaming. I'm not usually like that mister, really I'm not, I love my kids they are all I've got but if someone doesn't stop these blokes pestering me I'm going to explode.[9]

The fact that the majority of prisoners reside in the poorer districts has already been noted.[10] It is not surprising therefore that prisoners' families are themselves subject to a high degree of victimisation.[11] Men in prison are frequently worried about the safety of their home and belongings, however humble, and this fear is often justified. Whilst one man was in custody for a year his home was burgled fourteen times. The place was gradually stripped of practically everything. When the distraught wife was asked why she never reported it to the police she replied, 'With him inside for theft the Bill would just laugh at me, anyway he [her husband] wouldn't want me to, he doesn't trust them'.[12] Many other examples of prisoners' homes being burgled came to light. Seldom were they reported to the police; when they were it was usually as a result of pressure from a probation officer.

Women with their menfolk in prison suffer from the suspicion that they were quite content to live off the proceeds of crime whilst the man was at liberty but then turn to the social welfare organisations when he is caught. Whilst this is certainly justifiable criticism of a few women, it is highly doubtful if very many fit this pattern. Even if they did, does it justify denying aid to the children?

Some men in prison worry very much about the well-being of their children. Many express a concern for what the separation is doing to the child but as a prison chaplain explained:

In the main, the anxiety is a selfishly motivated thing and uses the child as a reason 'why I should be given parole' or 'why I should be given additional visiting facilities to see my child more frequently.' However, there are a few more genuine cases where the real concern is for the child. This is where the child, feeling isolated, first refuses any discipline from the mother, possibly refuses to eat and in some instances commits crime with the idea that it will then be imprisoned with his father. On one occasion we had a lad of eleven years of age who ran away from home and tried to break into the prison because he wanted to be with his father.[13]

The men in the two Leicester samples were asked to identify the main problems caused by imprisonment. The wives or cohabitees who were also interviewed were asked an identical question. The results are interesting. Forty-one per cent of the men in samples A and B combined gave self-centred replies, 29 per cent gave family-focused replies, 28 per cent had no problems and 2 per cent did not answer. These figures contrasted sharply with those obtained from the corresponding women. The wives and cohabitees whose partners had been surveyed saw the problems caused by imprisonment as hitting them and their children. There was an almost 100 per cent acceptance from the women that their man was 'all right inside'. Problems voiced by the women included disciplining the children, fretting children and babies, not knowing what to say to the children, loneliness, fear, frustration, stigma and some practical things like an inability to mend the broken washing machine. The men were mainly concerned with matters associated with the prison such as lack of privacy, employment after release, frequency of visits and mail. When a prisoner gave as his problem 'can't see the kids often enough' it was not always possible to separate whether this referred to his needs or theirs.

One point stands out clearly: it is not possible to identify a family's needs from what a prisoner chooses to tell a member of prison staff. Concerned men often ask for someone to visit their wife and children lest she be unable to cope. In most of such cases reported, the woman had a good support system. Some other cases where the man was reluctant to have anyone visit his family the woman was found to be in dire straights. The value of a home-visiting scheme, such as exists in Leicester, whereby a woman receives a visit from a volunteer within a day or two of her partner's imprisonment has therefore much to commend it. This point is pursued in Chapter 8.

Substitute men

Colin Copley threw some light on the extent to which women aquire a substitute during their husband's incarceration. In his sample 23 per cent reported taking another man. Copley suggests that a man may even encourage his wife to reject him for a while and take a substitute for herself during custody as part of his punishment. This acceptance of a wife's infidelity, says Copley, 'is accompanied by the contrary reaction of severe anger at the thought of the wife messing around. Many men express these contrasting emotions during their sentence. They will insist that their wives remain faithful to them throughout sentence, whilst freely admitting their own unfaithfulness when they were together. The relationship is viewed with rose-coloured affection, although it was often a stormy and unstable affair in reality.' Copley suggests, 'Throughout all these contradictions and flights of fantasy the man is expressing his fear of further rejection and future loss of meaningful relationships and acceptance. The process of separation forces him to re-assess and re-evaluate his status as husband and father within the family group and also his position in the social strata of the wider community.'[14]

Of course some women find another man when their husband is in prison in the same way they might if he was not. These liaisons may result in permanent relationships leading to the termination of the existing marriage or cohabitation. However, some women acquire a substitute only for the duration of the sentence. There are various reasons for this. Reference has already been made to the extent to which women can be pestered by men when their husbands are in prison. Cases have been identified where women selected a man with the deliberate intention of freeing themselves from the others. It appears that once a woman is 'fixed up' most of the serious pestering ceases. Others, especially those who reside in crime-prone neighbourhoods, will take a man for the physical or psychological protection his presence affords. On a more simple level, sexual frustration or just plain loneliness was given as the reason. Morris reported that prisoners' wives frequently mentioned the problem of sexual deprivation.[15] In some districts, a woman without a man lacks status. Perhaps this pressure is also a factor.

For whatever the reason a particular woman takes a substitute during her partner's imprisonment, difficulties can arise which in turn may impinge on any existing children. Copley found that in 14 per cent of his cases where the relationship between the prisoner and his wife was improved at the end of the sentence, the wife had taken a substitute. However, where the relationship had deteriorated, the wife had taken a substitute in 49 per cent of cases. It should not be assumed from this that the acquisition of a substitute had necessarily influenced the relationship one way or the other; but the figures are interesting. Health visitors reported a concern on the part of some women that they might become pregnant whilst their man was inside. Some women are reluctant to be seen at family planning clinics or seek contraception from their doctor while their husband is in prison. Health visitors obviously have an important role to play in this respect.

The response of any existing children to a 'substitute father' varies with the age of the child, his previous experience and other factors. Some resent the intruder and attempt to play him off against the mother. All must wonder to a certain extent and come to their own conclusions about what, if anything, they have been told. One little boy who had been told that his father was in hospital and that the man in the house was his mother's brother poured his heart out to his teacher at school, saying, 'Mummy has put Daddy in prison and is having incest with uncle'. In this instance the woman's efforts to protect her child from the truth misfired horribly.[16]

The various problems which women experience when their partner is sent to prison are such that some will take a temporary substitute. How this is explained to the child is of crucial importance to the dynamics of the family and the healthy development of its younger members.

Father's imprisonment as family therapy

Instances were described, particularly by teachers and voluntary workers, where a family flourished when a profligate, spendthrift father was locked away. Typical of many was this case described by a worker with a voluntary agency:

> The family was at breaking point up to the period of his remand. There were unpaid bills and threats that some of the services would be disconnected. Money was not available for essentials—unless you include the pub as one. During the few months he was on remand the wife paid off all the arrears on the rent and sorted out the gas and electricity. Mercifully (for the four children), the judge gave him another three years so we've no worries for a while so far as the kids are concerned. They are better fed, better clothed and get their sleep. But would you believe it, the silly b—— [the wife] can't wait to have the s—— back home.[17]

In contrast to such cases and those where 'absence makes the heart grow fonder', which delay or prevent a woman leaving an unsatisfactory relationship, some women are able to use the period of their partner's incarceration to effect a permanent separation. Much has been said and written by penal reformers and others about the tendency of imprisonment to cause family breakdown. There is, however, little hard evidence to substantiate it. One must also question whether divorce is always and inevitably bad for the children.

Evidence from the Leicester samples and from correspondents pointed to the fact that some men have a damaging effect on their wives and children which far outweighs any paternal value their presence in the family can offer.[18] In such cases permanent separation can remove a selfish, violent, cruel or habitually-drunken father from the orbit of his family. Not only can this have direct benefits for the children but its consequent effect on the mother improves her interaction with them and the care she is able to offer.

For a variety of reasons associated with fear, pressure and maintenance of the *status quo*, some women are unable to make the break whilst the man is with them. Others only recognise how different things could be without him when he is in prison. Yet others use his imprisonment as the reason for seeking divorce. People who care for the wife, such as parents and friends, may use a man's imprisonment as a reason to encourage her to leave him.

It is ironic that frequently women who escape from a damaging liaison then inflict a similar one on themselves and their children with their next relationship. Sixteen per cent of the Leicester samples of women with children were known to have had previous relationships with men who had been imprisoned. A further 21 per cent did not answer this question. In one case known to the author (but not in the Leicester or Bedford samples) a personable and attractive woman in her late thirties, with two children, divorced her husband after years of abuse and physical assaults associated with his excessive drinking. After living alone with her children for about three years she met another man, who within a few weeks was remanded in custody in connection with a great number of very serious offences against defenceless people. Neither the publicity given to the case in the national press, nor his complete disregard for the suffering he had caused, altered the woman's feelings towards him. They married whilst he was in prison serving a long sentence.

During the course of this study many cases came to light where a woman who had previously suffered at the hands of her husband or cohabitee launched herself into a new relationship with a man about whom she knew little, apart from his criminal record. Others married men who had assaulted them in the past. In most of these cases children were involved and therefore brought into the new and uncertain relationships.

Some families survive on a knife's edge, very much in need of help but not referred to social services. Others refuse welfare provision—apart from money—because they are hostile to authority or suspicious of the motive of the health visitor, probation officer or social worker. In cases where it is the man who resists or is antagonistic and where that resistance has not been overcome, his imprisonment can provide the rest of the family with an opportunity to benefit from advice and counselling. Teachers reported an improvement in some children when their fathers were sent to prison.[19]

Like any other enforced absence of a father, imprisonment can provide an opportunity for a boy in a family to mature and test out his responsibilities in a way which may have been deprived him in the past. It is a common occurrence for the eldest son of a prisoner to become the head of the family and for this to be welcomed by the mother. Depending upon the length of the sentence such a development may store up problems for the man's return when he seeks once more to resume his role.

It is important to make it clear that nothing contained in this section should be taken to imply that most prisoners are necessarily bad or unloving fathers and husbands. However, some are, and for their children and wives the period of imprisonment can provide a respite or a chance to separate permanently.

Notes

1 Matthews, Jill (1983).
2 Philips, Kate (1985); this extensive extract is quoted by kind permission of its author and *Nursing Mirror* in which her original article was published.
3 See also Chapter 2.
4 Reported in NACRO *New Digest* Number 39, June 1986.
5 Personal correspondence.
6 Large numbers of men are imprisoned without them or their families having any contact with the probation service, for instance, fine defaulters and those remanded in custody. Additionally, a significant number are sent to prison without the court calling for a social inquiry report. See Chapter 2.
7 See Chapter 8 and also Appendix A.
8 Letter from a prisoner's wife.
9 Interview with a prisoner's wife.
10 *Ibid*; Chapter 1.
11 The Home Office (1986) Crime Prevention Unit states in its booklet *Crime Prevention and the Community Programme*, 'On some of the poorest housing estates, for example, every year at least one in every eight households will be burgled, on some very disadvantaged estates, one in three. The national average is around one in forty.' Using data from the British Crime Survey, Hope (1986) showed that the higher risk of burglary in poor council estates was also accompanied by a higher fear of crime.
12 Interview with a prisoner's wife.
13 Personal correspondence.
14 Copley, C. (1981) The author is indebted to the Rev. Dr Colin Copley, Assistant Chaplain General, H.M. Prison Service, for a copy of his unpublished work on the effects of imprisonment on family relationships.
15 Morris, P. (1965).
16 Interview with a teacher.
17 Personal correspondence.
18 The same probably applies to women and also to non-prisoners of both sexes.
19 See Chapter 5.

4

The Prisoner's Child and His Family

What are children told?

Cindy, eight years old, stood apprehensively at the window. 'When's Daddy coming home?' she whined. There was no reply from her mother who was tidying up, or rather moving things from one place to another in a mindless fashion. 'Why hasn't Daddy come home?' repeated the same little voice as its owner peeped through the curtains into the growing dusk outside. Again no answer was forthcoming. A greater sense of urgency became apparent in the raised pitch of the little voice. 'Mummy, why isn't Daddy home, is he all right? What's happened, Mummy? Where's Daddy?' The distraught woman rounded on her child. 'He's not coming home, don't you understand?', she screamed. 'Just shut up, will you, shut up!' Cindy stood absolutely still for a second or two and then ran screaming from the room as her mother broke down and sobbed bitterly.

This incident was actually witnessed by the author but a number of correspondents and workers mentioned similar examples, and described the problems which result when a woman is unable to face her child with the unpalatable truth about the father's absence. A child's fantasies are such that an event of this kind can lead to a great variety of extreme reasons being invented and turned over in his mind. 'If mother won't tell me, something terrible must have happened!' In reality, the man may only have been locked up for a few days or weeks but to the child with no information and a mother who is unable to talk about it, he may as well have disappeared for ever.

More frequently a child is told lies, either to protect him from the unpleasant reality or because the mother cannot or will not tell him the truth. The Leicester study suggested that the most common reason offered for father's absence was that he was either working away from home or looking for a job. Whilst this may well satisfy many children in the short term, the long-term difficulties are considerable. If the matter was reported in the press there is a strong likelihood that someone will mention it to the child. In areas with a high crime rate there is always a distinct possibility that the prison grapevine will pass information out of the prison on a visit. Thus a child visiting his father may hear that the father of a classmate has been imprisoned; it is then extremely unlikely that such a juicy piece of news will not be passed around at school.[1]

In cases where the family does succeed in keeping the father's imprisonment a secret from the children, the question arises as to when, if ever, they will be told. When asked this question some parents were adamant. 'Never', they said. Others said the children would be told the truth, 'when they are old enough' or 'when the time is right'. One is forced to ponder when that might be. There is considerable literature on adoption to suggest that the sudden imparting of information of great personal and emotional import is a very serious matter and can have far-reaching consequences.[2] Instances were described by correspondents in which the mother had woven a complex fabric of lies, involving friends and relations, to conceal the truth. As prisoners are allowed to write to children on paper not bearing the prison address, this is possible.

What a child is told depends to some extent on his age. Some were told that their fathers were helping Father Christmas; the child of a man on remand was informed that his father had 'gone to buy him a new BMX', a boy of Asian background believed his father had gone back to Pakistan. In other words a range of explanations were discovered which bore out the experiences of other researchers.

Among the many reasons found to have been given to children to explain father's absence were some of a particularly imaginative nature. One child was told that his father was in prison because he was 'working undercover for the police'. As far as could be ascertained from observation at visits, the child had swallowed this. He no doubt saw his father as a hero, a sort of James Bond. One wonders how long the family will keep up the story and what the child's reaction will be when he discovers the truth—always assuming, of course, that the man was *not* an undercover police officer!

The Leicester samples disclosed instances of children in the same family being told different things to explain their fathers' absence. In a number of cases an older child in his early teens was made guardian of the truth and told his father was in prison. A child a few years younger was told the man was working away, whilst five- and six-year olds were judged too young to understand or told nothing at all.[3] The pressure which such information puts on the older child must be considerable and research into this and its effects on the family dynamics is called for.

A child does not suddenly reach an age at which he fully understands the meaning of imprisonment. Therefore the arbitrary decisions of some parents to decide that their child is 'too young to understand' give rise to all sorts of anomalies. Conversations about the father often take place in the child's presence. Sometimes the fact that the man is in prison is discussed freely even though the child has been told that his father is working away or been given some other excuse. Numerous examples were discovered and have been quoted by other authors in which a child is told he is visiting his father at his place of work or even in a hospital, only for the youngster to read 'HM Prison' on the gate or to learn the truth from elsewhere.[4]

In both the Leicester samples 36 per cent of the children who were in the care of the prisoner's wife or cohabitee were said to have been told the truth but in the case of the miners' children it was 59 per cent. The small Bedford sample showed a figure of 35 per cent. These figures support Morris's conclusion that a substantial number of prisoners' children are unaware that their father is in prison, 38 per cent in her study.[5] The findings also equate exactly with Monger and Pendleton whose Nottingham mothers could be divided equally between those who told their children and those who did not; 36 per cent of each with the remainder unrecorded.[6] Wilmer found 36 per cent where the children were not told,[7] but Copley records a lower figure, 23 per cent, which he attributed to 'the consequence of improved visiting facilities in prisons for families where children can now be taken to meet their fathers in reasonably pleasant surroundings and use special play areas to mix with other children during the visit.'[8] In this respect it is important to bear in mind that the two Leicester and the Bedford samples were from very busy, cramped and overcrowded establishments where the visiting facilities and the time allowed were far from ideal.[9] The samples were also of men just received into the prison; a survey of men in training prisons might well produce different results. As has been mentioned earlier, the men studied were not sentenced to more than six months and there is a greater incentive to hide the truth if the father is to be back with the family within a few days or weeks. The proportion of children considered 'too young to understand', and therefore not told of their fathers' imprisonment was between 11 and 12 per cent in all three samples. Some men did not know what, if anything, their children would be told. Many of these inmates were those suddenly or unexpectedly imprisoned, for instance fine defaulters.

In some cases children who are told the truth may be too young to comprehend its meaning—perhaps they are still infants. In instances where this happened the mother took the view that the child should grow up knowing what had happened and not suddenly learn about it from elsewhere in later life.

In the majority of cases where the wife or cohabitee was interviewed, it was found that what she had told the children corresponded with what the prisoner had said in his questionnaire. However, in a few cases the parents were overtaken by events, namely publicity given to the case, following which a decision not to tell the child was reversed.

Thus it can be seen that whilst many children do not know their fathers' whereabouts, a sizeable proportion are told the truth. The truth, however, can take many forms and it is doubtful if all the explanations are necessarily in the long-term interests of the child. Examples of how the news was imparted by some mothers in areas of high crime and delinquency included: 'The bobbies have taken him away'; 'the bobbies have got him and locked him up' and more strongly still 'the pigs have fitted your Dad up' and 'his mates grassed on him'. A far higher proportion of miners imprisoned for incidents arising out of the coal strike indicated that their children had been told the truth, but here again the fact was sometimes put in an emotional way such as saying that a man was 'imprisoned for fighting for the right to work'.

Whether or not parents tell their children the truth, the way in which they communicate with them and how they explain father's absence is arguably one of the most important factors of imprisonment over which they have some control. This will be discussed further in Chapter 8.

Children's reactions

A volunteer worker described the following case:

> Keith is a very bright and inquisitive three-year-old whose father was sentenced to twelve months' imprisonment in October. He started to attend the playgroup in March and seemed to get a lot of enjoyment from it. He fitted in well with the other children and joined in all the games. In May, Keith's father was released. The following week this conversation took place:
>
> *Keith*: Do you know where my father lives?
> *Worker*: He lives at home with you and your family.
> *Keith*: No, he lives in the police station.
> *Worker*: He's back at home now with you all.
> *Keith*: He won't stay with us. He lives at the police station.
>
> Since his father's release, Keith's behaviour at the playgroup has become erratic. He has punched the other children on several occasions and appears to be generally unhappy.[10]

This was an unusual case but it is by no means rare for some children to be conditioned to the regular disappearance of their father into prison. Some children take such an experience as a normal part of living and display no obvious ill-effects. Some positively bloom when a violent, selfish or hurtful member of the family is taken away for a while. Others display considerable emotional and physical upset. Reports were received of children running away, some 'disappearing', although they were only ten to twelve years of age. Some women gave as a reason for not telling children their father was in prison the fear that they might run away; some said they had done so on previous occasions. Two health visitors reported that some children felt unsafe in the company of their mother alone.[11] A prison chaplain stated, 'Not a few prisoners have told me that their children have received some comfort from being told that Dad is in the sort of situation that Godber is, in the television series *Porridge*.'

There is great variation in the way in which children cope with the fact that their father is in prison. Whilst for some it is a normal occurrence and for a few a relief, for others it can be very traumatic. Instances were described where youngsters became hysterical, depressive or delinquent. Others engaged in a systematic 'hate campaign' to all who came near. A prison chaplain described how a little girl at a London prison was able to cope with the fact that her father went behind the netting and bars into the prison by seeing his position as analogous to that of her pet budgerigar.

Thus it can be seen that there is no typical case, no common set of circumstances which prevail when a father goes away. Every family is different and these differences are amplified by personal idiosyncrasies, by the availability or otherwise of support from friends and family and by social class. At one end of the class continuum is the child from a high crime area where imprisonment of a father and brother is a common occurrence amongst peers, at the other end, the middle-class child of previous happy experience where the father's incarceration attacks status, career prospects, self-image and loving attention.[12]

The vast majority of women who were interviewed, and teachers, health visitors and others who reported, saw imprisonment of a father as detrimental to many children and sometimes giving rise to serious consequences such as failure to thrive, ill health, disturbed behaviour, truancy and lowered school performance, regardless of the social class or economic group of the family. Bed-wetting from an otherwise dry child and reduced concentration were the more common of the minor and perhaps expected symptoms. These findings equate with those of Friedman and Esselstyn who, more than twenty years ago, observed, 'There is more than suggestive evidence here that committing a father to jail is soon accompanied by a depression in the school performance of his children—not only academically, but in all other particulars as well. The link between the jail commitment of the father as breadwinner and the financial problems of his wife has long been known. It is now time to explore the link between jail confinement and the education of their young.' They added, 'It is also striking, although the numbers involved are small, that girls seem to be more adversely influenced than boys . . . there is clear evidence of greater damage in the girl when the father is committed and thus one might well assume that if a father is committed to jail, his daughter needs expert guidance immediately.'[13]

Father's crime and his child

There is far from universal agreement that the perpetrators of the majority of offences should be locked up.[14] Yet a prison sentence is generally recognised as the most severe penalty and as such it can heighten a child's perception of the gravity of his father's crime, even if the offence was relatively trivial. Some of the uninformed public, of which the prisoner's child may be part, may believe that those who go to prison are chiefly killers, rapists, vicious and violent thugs and muggers of the lame and elderly. Even the most cursory look at the official figures will dispel this myth.[15] The prisoner's child, however, does not consult the official figures. If the reason for the father's imprisonment is not explained and discussed with the child, as it frequently is not, the child is left to dwell on it. He wonders what terrible deed his father has done to bring down on him the most severe penalty open to the State. Whether such an event influences the child's attitude towards his father's behaviour is a subject about which we know little although there is some evidence that sentences do not affect adult public disapproval.[16] Many children do know what their father did. In these cases their reaction will be influenced by their previous experiences in life, the sub-culture in which they live and the relationship they have with their parents. For many, the removal of the father to prison is a relatively common occurrence, not only to them but also to their friends and peers. For others it is a step into the unknown, a move into darkness.

Some offences are particularly serious or give rise to greater than average public disapproval. In these cases the nature of the criminal act, rather than the incarceration of the father, may be the principal burden the child has to bear. A probation officer working in a maximum security prison wrote:

> Suppose a man who has never been to prison before is convicted of a serious offence on a close member of his family for whom he had shown no strong feelings of antagonism before. He is sent to prison for a long time. The children are left in the care of adults with their own feelings about the crime, the culprit, the victim and the additional responsibility thrust upon them. The feelings the children have about the loss of their father are compounded by their vulnerability and need for security. They must be sensitive to the feelings of their guardians and the need to avoid the risk of losing them, too. If the guardians are hostile towards the father, the children may well feel that it is in their best interests to claim to reject him too.[17]

A small number of offences are committed on victims within the family. The consequences of such crimes can be enormous. A correspondent described one such case in which a man killed his wife after discovering she was having an affair with another man. The correspondent, a prison probation officer, concluded her lengthy description of the case as follows:

> The need for the children to have help in making sense of what had happened to them was largely overlooked or acknowledged as being secondary to their physical needs. Sadly, the children learned to adapt and conceal feelings that were not welcome or understood. The father returned in a relatively short period of time [18 months] to his family but for the children that time was too long, given that he was the only one apparently able to recognise and respond to their emotional needs.[18]

Another case which also involved a man killing his wife was described by a member of Dr Barnardo's staff:

> A family of five children came into the care of Barnardo's in 1966. It consisted of Donald aged about six, Charles of seven-and-a-half and Larry of eight-and-a-half; one girl, Janet, aged nine-and-a-half and the eldest boy Paul, then aged about eleven. Prior to coming the family had experienced a traumatic life. Father strangled mother, was remanded in custody, convicted of manslaughter and released from custody following sentence. Some time later he met and married another woman and had a child by her. Before long, she too was strangled to death. Once again he was convicted of manslaughter but this time was sentenced to life imprisonment. The children were split between grandparents and an aunt but their disturbed behaviour led to them being taken into residential care.
>
> Efforts were made to keep the children together but with such a large family this produced difficulties. All five remained in a Dr Barnardo's home throughout their childhood; the three younger boys living with the family of a member of the staff. Neither the children nor the staff knew all the details of their family background.
>
> A psychiatrist involved with the case believed that the children should maintain contact with their father 'for ever'. As a result, every six weeks all five were taken by car to Wormwood Scrubs from one of the London suburbs. This proved to be a harrowing and traumatic experience which lasted for many years. The member of staff involved feels that in retrospect this was not in the children's best interests. As the years passed the five all showed different symptoms of disturbed behaviour, some being in trouble with the law. Nevertheless they all maintained links with their 'foster father' at Barnardo's although the relationship was sometimes turbulent.
>
> When he was twenty years of age Charles was killed in a motor cycle accident. The remaining children are still in contact with their natural father who has now served about twenty years in prison. There are occasional talks about the possibility of his being paroled.

Paul is now in his second cohabitation with a child from each. He has maintained a regular work pattern.

Janet has had one, sometimes turbulent, relationship and has a son aged about ten.

Larry married recently and has a child following a relationship of some four or five years' standing.

Donald married in 1984 a girl he first went out with when he was thirteen. The couple lived together for at least four years.[19]

This case illustrates the way attitudes to how children should be treated have changed over twenty years. The modern idea would be to tell them as much of the truth as possible but in a positive manner, drawing on the good things from their past and the good things that were known of their parents. 'Life story work', as it is called, is an important ingredient in the management of children who have suffered from the break-up of their family, for whatever reason. Imprisonment of the father and the offence which he committed are important parts of the story. When the victim is the children's own mother, the difficulties are amplified.

Occasionally the child may himself have been the father's victim— battered, sexually assaulted or otherwise abused. He may or may not feel betrayed or wounded by his father's actions. The removal of the father may impose a period of peace and calm in the life of the child; on the other hand it may amplify and compound the confusion and insecurity. Both the Leicester samples and correspondence from elsewhere in the country suggested that escalation of problems was a frequent occurrence following imprisonment. When the offence was committed against a child in the offender's home, the man's release from prison at the end of his sentence can give rise to further upheavals. Not only will the family have to come to terms with his release but also the official concern for the safety of the child, coupled no doubt with a desire to safeguard their own position, can lead the social services departments to consider removing the child from home. The child is in this way being treated as if he were a delinquent.

The Howard League Working Party on Unlawful Sex made the point:

Juvenile victims of sex offences of all kinds are already substantial-ly protected by s.39 of the Children and Young Persons Act, 1933, (as amended by s.57(4) of the Children and Young Persons Act, 1963), whereby the courts can prohibit publication of 'any particulars calculated to lead to the identification of any child or young person'. If, however, a court fails to make such an order—in an incest case for example—the press are free to publish the offender's name, thus making known the child's involvement to neighbours and schoolfel-lows, with consequences that can all too easily be imagined, not least at the hands of their schoolfriends' parents, who may forbid them to have any contact with the child. To give just one example, in 1981 a

Northamptonshire newspaper gave the name and address of a man convicted of sexual assaults over a twelve month period on a girl of twelve. It was not mentioned that she was in fact his daughter, but the information was quite enough to identify her to schoolfellows and neighbours. According to social workers' records, the family received abusive telephone calls, the mother was rejected by neighbours because she allowed her husband back, and the girl did not return to her school because of the publicity.[20]

We have seen that the more lurid and gross crimes, and those committed by the middle class or men not usually engaged in criminal behaviour may weigh heavily on a child's mind. However, a very large proportion of prisoners' children reside in the poorest areas of town and cities. Here the sub-cultural influences produce an attitude to violence, loyalty and honesty which condone or even applaud some types of assault and thieving. In these instances imprisonment of a father is often described to the child as the fault of others rather than the result of his anti-social behaviour. In such cases one effect of the sentence on the child may be to reinforce parental attitudes and is a further reason to hate the police and the 'establishment'.

The orphans of justice

Among the more critical situations which can develop is one in which the imprisoned man is head of a single-parent family. The Leicester sample contained three such cases. In percentage terms the figure is not very high but numerically the problem is not insignificant, given the high use of imprisonment. Staff of children's homes made this point and some spoke at length about the hardship it created for the children. Unlike imprisoned mothers, where such an event is not uncommon and is therefore given some attention, male offenders who have sole responsibility for their children are seldom the subject of debate. Nevertheless, they exist. One described case involved children of different sexes being removed from their home following the imprisonment of their father. They were then placed in different institutions and as a result lost everything near to them, their father, their home and each other.[21] The confusion and despair they may have experienced can only be imagined; in this example the children might have felt, with some justification, that to be removed from home and placed in an institution as if they were the criminals was a severe punishment and one which was quite undeserved. In other reported cases, friends, family or neighbours took charge of children following the imprisonment of their single-parent father.

One of the most alarming aspects of these situations is that it is possible for a man to be brought to court and imprisoned, or taken to a

prison by the police, without the appropriate agencies (such as probation and social services) being aware of what is happening or alerted to
the fact that he has sole care of a child.[22]

Although the extreme case of a child being orphaned by his parent's
imprisonment is not very common, loss of a child's only *able* parent is
more frequent. It is not possible to quantify this on the basis of the
Leicester samples but a sufficient number of cases were brought to light
by health visitors, specialist social workers, prison chaplains and
teachers to suggest that this is a matter of some gravity. Cases were
described where, because of physical or mental illness, low intellect,
absence of social skills or lack of maternal feeling, the mother was
unable to cope without her partner. In some of these instances the family
collapsed, whilst in others it was only held together by considerable
input from social and community health services, probation, and other
statutory or voluntary bodies.

Teachers spoke of children being kept away from school when the
father was in prison.[23] A prison chaplain described a 14-year-old girl
of Asian origin kept at home to help in the family business in order that
it could survive the father's nine-month prison sentence. The business
was a general store and the man's wife could not speak English.[24]

A number of health visitors observed the expanding role of fathers in
the care of infants and young children. Even only a few years ago,
particularly in working class districts, it was quite rare for a health
visitor to meet a father, either at the family's home or at a clinic.
Nowadays, due partly to changing attitudes but largely to the massive
escalation of unemployment in poor socio-economic areas, the trend is
changing. The father is more frequently encountered at home by the
health visitor, and he may even bring his baby to the clinic for check-ups
and vaccinations.[25] These fathers clearly have a greater involvement in
attending to the needs of their very young children than was previously
the case. Whilst there are obvious advantages in this trend, it com-
pounds the family difficulties still further when he is sent to prison. This
is particularly so in those cases where the woman is less than adequate in
ministering to the needs of her infant. This is discussed further in
Chapters 5 and 8.

Myrna Rourke in a paper to the International Primary Health Care
Conference observed, 'In today's world, mothers of toddlers experience
stress in their everyday world, not just in crisis. When mothers are faced
with demands straining their ability to cope, their responses depend
upon their internal and external environments. Support systems,
including significant others, housing, economic security and community
resources, reflect external environment, while feelings, self concept,
attitudes and emotions are internal factors. The mother with an
attentive, concerned husband, an extended family and family security
may find coping with an irritable toddler not to be unmanageable,
whereas a mother with a frequently-absent husband, no extended family

or other social supports and no financial security may find it most difficult. It may require the addition of only a minor stressor, such as a late payday, to create a crisis.'[26]

Many prisoners' families have all the stressors described by Rourke—and a great many more besides. Rourke was concerned with toddlers, however; when the children are older, other difficulties emerge, as any parent knows. Wilson described the part played by the family in shaping children's behaviour, particularly in relation to delinquency.[27] Wallerstein, reporting on a ten-year follow-up of children of divorced parents, observed, 'Some youngsters showed intense yearning and compassionate caring for troubled, needy fathers who showed up erratically over the years . . . . A heightened need to establish relationships with absent fathers appeared to occur as these youngsters, especially the girls, reached adolescence.'[28]

There are occasions when the father, though in prison, exerts great influence over a child—especially when there is no mother. Such a situation raises a considerable dilemma for social workers. The rights of both father and child, and the wishes and best interests of the child all appear to be in conflict. The following example from a probation officer illustrates this problem:

> Sally is nine years old and has been in local authority care for two years since her father was sentenced to 12 years' imprisonment. She is taken by her social worker to see her father every month. The week before the visit she is excitable and anxious and gets little sleep. The week after the visit is a winding down process during which she is most unpredictable. She has run away from the home several times, without having much idea where she is running to. Her father writes three or four times a week just repeating the sentiment that 'Daddy loves his little girl'. Two foster homes have broken down because of pressure from him.'[29]

The fact that some women are unable to cope—through no fault of their own—must be kept in perspective; a number cope extremely well; some better than when their partner is at liberty.

Non-parent fathers

The Leicester samples provided an insight into the number of men received into prison who had children for whom they no longer took, or had never taken responsibility.[30] Many knew nothing of their children's present whereabouts. Some inmates have an attitude to women, sex and paternal responsibility which reduces their effectiveness as fathers. To a certain extent this is symptomatic of the low socio-economic and educationally deprived environment from which they emanate, coupled with their own family life experience. To what extent imprisonment increases this is not known, but the attitude to women exhibited in prisons generally, by staff and inmates alike, coupled with the artificially tough and macho image which a proportion of both try to develop, cannot help.

Thus once again the children of imprisoned fathers can be identified at the bottom of the 'pecking order', as one of the most deprived if not the most deprived group in our society. It is of course possible that a proportion of these children will eventually be fostered, adopted or otherwise cared for and in this way benefit from their father's absence. However, the child's life experience up to that point might have been such that his aggressive and disturbed behaviour mediated against a successful placement. Cases were described in which attempts to foster such children broke down because their behaviour was so destructive to all concerned.[31] On the other hand some placements were very successful, with the child fitting in well to the new environment. A great number, nevertheless, remain in children's homes and in the care of local authorities.[32]

Some prisoners with children are themselves very young. Although this book refers largely to the children of male prisoners aged twenty-one and over, the comments of a chaplain of a Youth Custody Centre are of interest:

Attitudes among the fathers of the inmate population vary enormously, although on the whole they seem to care about the welfare of their children. However, their understanding of the appropriate way in which to care often leaves a lot to be desired. One area which they often feel is of no real significance is that of their presence within the family unit. It seems too easy for them to opt out of responsibilities believing that mother can not only cope but they themselves are merely providers (the State of course providing in their absence).

About 6 per cent of inmates in that particular chaplain's Youth Custody Centre had one or more children.[33]

The normal child

Much has been said about the problems which children exhibit when subjected to trauma such as the imprisonment of their father. It is therefore of some importance to put the matter into perspective and to keep in mind the fact that all children, even those brought up in the best possible atmosphere and in relatively trouble-free families throw tantrums, become sullen and in many other ways cause worry to their parents. Readers of this book are urged to remember this and not to assume that a child's temporary bad behaviour or changing mood is necessarily the result of 'damage' following a father's removal to prison.

Teachers and others carrying out their professional duties will no doubt recognise this; they are not emotionally involved with the child. A parent, however, certainly is emotionally involved where his or her own child is concerned and therefore may not be able to stand back to consider the child's behaviour objectively. Parents who read this book and are in the situation where the father has been sent to prison may have difficulty in deciding if their child's behaviour is normal, a natural response to father's absence (which is perhaps healthy) or an exaggerated, unhealthy reaction where advice should be sought. For parents in this position there are a number of books which throw some light on the behaviour of children, demonstrating that 'normal', healthy boys and girls do frequently behave in ways that are alarming to their parents. Two books are especially recommended; both are inexpensive. Details of both are given in the footnotes at the end of this chapter and in the Bibliography.[34]

It is surprising what children can take in their stride; it is also surprising what little things hurt and worry them. The potential for harm *can* be reduced, as has been described earlier in this book in references related to divorce and separation. A prison chaplain observed:

I believe that on the whole children are pretty resilient; as children they attract love and they give it. If their father has been or is in prison, it of course must have an effect on them. I do not think this effect is altogether negative. If a man is doing a short sentence, the effect of the sentence may bring the family more closely together and assist in helping them realise the value of family unity. If the family unit breaks down there are others who will take the place of the imprisoned man. If the man is in prison for a long sentence, then there is usually a good reason why this has occurred. The family may stay together and the stronger the attachments the more likely this will succeed.[35]

It would be incorrect to suppose that all the problems caused by a father's imprisonment can be solved simply by open, considerate discussion between parents and children in a warm, loving family; numerous examples quoted in this book show this all too clearly. Similarly it would be wrong to attribute all a child's bad behaviour to the imprisonment of his father. These things should be kept in perspective.

Notes

1 See Chapter 5.
2 There is much literature on this subject but see, for example, Raynor (1980).
3 This corresponds with the findings of other research, for instance Morris

(1965), Wilmer [quoted by Monger and Pendleton (1981)], Copley (1981), Monger (1970).
4 See for instance Monger and Pendleton op.cit.; Morris (1967).
5 Morris op.cit.
6 Monger and Pendleton op.cit.
7 Wilmer op.cit.
8 Copley op.cit.
9 Visiting facilities in HMP Leicester are now much improved but still not sufficiently adequate to allow for the frequency and length of visit permitted in some training prisons. This is due to several factors, the very small size of the prison site being the most significant. The great priority given to escort duties to courts, and security considerations also have an effect.
10 Personal correspondence.
11 Personal correspondence.
12 See also Chapter 5.
13 Friedman and Esselstyn (1965).
14 See Hough and Mayhew (1983) *British Crime Survey* also Shaw, S. (1982) in Shaw, Roger and Hutchison, Rita (eds) *Periodic Restriction of Liberty.*
15 Home Office (1985) *Prison Statistics England and Wales 1984.*
16 Walker and Marsh (1984).
17 Personal correspondence.
18 Personal correspondence.
19 Personal correspondence.
20 Howard League (1985) see also case described in Chapter 5.
21 Interview with residential social worker.
22 See cases described in Chapters 2 and 5.
23 Personal correspondence.
24 Personal correspondence.
25 Information gleaned from correspondence, case studies and interviews with health visitors.
26 Rourke, M.(1984).
27 Wilson, H.(1983).
28 Wallerstein, J.(1984) and see also Rutter, M. (1977).
29 Personal correspondence.
30 See Chapter 1 and Table 3.
31 Personal correspondence and interviews with residential staff.
32 Personal correspondence and interviews with residential staff.
33 Personal correspondence.
34 Spicer, F. (1977) *Adolescence and Stress* and Dunn, Judy (1984) *Sisters and Brothers.*
35 Personal correspondence.

5

The Prisoner's Child and The Outside World

The importance of the teacher

As a child grows and develops, factors outside the home become increasingly influential. Arguably the most important is the school, wherein the impact—for good or ill—of teachers and other children is considerable. The child who is unhappy, disturbed or hurt as a result of his father's imprisonment is in particular need of help and support at school, and is especially vulnerable to his needs being ignored, unrecognised or unmet.[1] These needs may be all the greater in cases where the remaining parent is for some reason unable to provide the necessary quality of care.[2] The consequence of this is that a great weight of responsibility falls to teachers because of their unique position. Other professionals whose training and ethos should enable them to respond to the needs of children of imprisoned fathers, such as probation officers and social workers, are systematically prevented from doing so and thus reach only a tiny proportion.[3] Education welfare officers are few in number and, like other social work professionals, reach only a selected proportion of prisoners' children. Teachers, however, reach all children—at least all who attend school—so responsibility falls to the teaching profession to decide whether or not to act. Lack of resources, financial constraints, difficulties in respect of confidentiality coupled with the fact that many children of imprisoned fathers are concentrated in schools with deprived inner-city districts and large council estates within their catchment areas, makes a decision to act a difficult one to take with sincerity.[4] A decision to take no action is surely just as difficult, given the social, moral and humanitarian factors involved and the deprived status of many of these children. Many prisoners' children have no other source of potential support outside or even inside their home. In other cases such support that does exist takes the form of judgemental attitudes, an awareness only of the child's material needs or else a collusion with the father's crime and a reinforcement of anti-police and anti-authoritarian attitudes.[5]

In discussions associated with this research, many teachers declared that they should not be expected to be social workers, they were not equipped for such a task and had inadequate resources even to carry out their existing duties adequately, let alone to take on the special needs of this large and difficult group of children. Others in education, many of them primary school teachers, argued that unhappiness is a barrier to learning which cannot be ignored. Some meetings addressed by the author revealed the powerful feelings that the issue provoked among teachers holding differing beliefs.

The decision facing teachers in respect of whether they should be active in providing help for this particular group of children is indeed a difficult one; as is the rider to it—if they don't, who does? Half a million children are involved so the question is not simply academic.[6] Some suggestions for possible action are made in the final chapter.

The remainder of this section is concerned with what emerged from the Leicester samples and from communications, including interviews, with teachers and others from different parts of the country.

Questionnaires were sent to the school heads of twenty-one teachers in respect of those children in the Leicester Prison sample whose mothers had consented. No reply was forthcoming from one, another wrote to explain that the problems associated with the teachers' dispute meant that he had few staff available and could not cooperate. One headteacher said she would only consider involvement with the consent of the Director of Education. Since the time scale did not permit such bureaucratic niceties, since only one child was involved and the remaining heads were prepared for their staff to cooperate, this case was not pursued.[7] Eighteen therefore responded and three were contacted at a later date after the children concerned had changed schools. The high response rate, 86 per cent, is seen as indicative of the interest and concern of teachers in this subject. Little information was forthcoming from a few of the questionnaires, because the school had known the child for a short time. In other cases, in addition to providing answers to given questions teachers gave further information about the child where they thought it was relevant. They also gave details and histories of other children of imprisoned fathers known to them in their professional capacity. For instance, on a questionnaire in which the answers indicated that the father's imprisonment had no apparent effect on the child, the headteacher wrote:

This information is not indicative of other experiences I have observed. In four other instances three boys have shown considerable distress and talked frequently about the situation. They all displayed behaviour problems during the period of internment. These boys were of infant age and knew where their father was. One girl became withdrawn; she was of nursery age and unaware of her father's situation.

The amount of information supplied by teachers is all the more impressive given that the survey was conducted during the height of the teachers' dispute (1984–85) when morale was at a low ebb; both headteachers and staff could easily have found valid reasons for not cooperating.

It is not the purpose of this short book to describe this part of the research in any detail–that will be done elsewhere.[8] We are concerned here with the relationship between the teacher and the prisoner's child, the difficulties which are presented and how the teacher sees his or her role. It must be emphasised that the sample is small and from one part of the country only. Nevertheless, what emerged was in keeping with the observations received from people inside and outside the teaching profession and from different parts of the country.

No formal procedures exist whereby schools are informed that a child's father has been sent into custody. Teachers find out—if they become aware of it at all, that is—through a variety of channels. Sometimes a child may confide in a member of the school staff, or the mother will tell a teacher. More frequently teachers hear from other children, piece it together from press reports or suspect what has happened from the child's behaviour coupled with knowledge of the family background.

Some teachers have considerable experience of children of imprisoned fathers because of the catchment area of the school; others have none. In some schools a child with an imprisoned father is a rare phenomenon and if known about can become the focus of attention. A probation officer and a mother described how a child was expelled from a private school following the imprisonment of his father. Fortunately numerous examples of the opposite reaction were described although not from private schools where the child was the subject of much support from school staff. In one case the school provided breakfast every morning while the father was away, in the knowledge that the mother was unable to cope and that meals at home would be irregular. However, perhaps the most important thing which a teacher can offer an unhappy child is time; time to talk and time which gives permission to talk. Sadly, where this is most needed it is a scarce commodity because of the clustering effect of problems in the most deprived districts. Many teachers, however, do take it upon themselves to spend time with children who need it and there is increasing recognition of the role of the teacher in respect of family problems.[9] Quite often, though, the school plays a passive role and does nothing in this respect unless the child actually asks for help. Several teachers justified this on the grounds that a child is entitled to privacy and should not be questioned. Such a view is challenged by the following case:

Peter was quite a bright little boy but what might be described as a late developer both physically and intellectually. It was a few days after his thirteenth birthday that the police came to take his father away. Peter understood what had happened and why. The family had talked about it at some length before the decision was made not to pay the fines for the road traffic offences. Peter's father had had a good job and had never been in trouble before apart from a speeding conviction. Unemployment struck when his firm closed down making him redundant. He had worked his way up to a managerial position on the basis of long service, hard work and ability and not because of any qualifications he could use elsewhere. Having to live on social security was very difficult and one of the things that suffered was the car. When stopped by the police the tax was out of date as was the MOT certificate and two tyres were below the legal limit. As if this wasn't bad enough they were stopped again, twice during the next two weeks, once going to visit the mother's sick father at home and then going to see him again in hospital shortly before he died. The total weight of fines imposed by the courts was such that Peter's father felt there was no way of paying them without rendering the financial situation of the family even worse. Husband and wife reluctantly took the grave decision that he would spend however many days in prison it meant to clear off the fines. He regretted having used the car illegally but justified this to himself and his family on the grounds that his wife needed to see her dying father. The boy understood this—as much as any thirteen year old can understand the reasons why prison is invoked in some cases and not others. The boy also felt he needed to keep it to himself; the family had indicated this was not the sort of thing one talked about.

Not many days had passed before one of the more infamous youths at Peter's school announced to all and sundry that Peter's dad was 'in the nick', without saying why or for how long. The impact of this on some of the other children, or possibly on their parents when they came to hear of it, was that they no longer sought Peter's company and friends he had associated with in the past played with other children. The youth who made the announcement, however, and some of his friends, many of whom had relations in prison, were quite happy to play with Peter and before long the lad's peer group had changed markedly from comparatively law-abiding children with caring parents to the more troublesome element in the school whose parents cared little about what their children did or else were not at liberty to do anything about it. Had Peter's mother confided in teachers at school things might have been different. As it was, school staff only came to hear of it late in the day from other children and then did not know how best to react or else felt Peter was entitled to his own privacy.

It was not very long before Peter was arrested for being lookout when a house close to the school was burgled. He was adamant that he had learned his lesson, that he had been foolish, had been led astray and that such a thing would never happen again. Since it was his first offence and because it was police policy to caution juveniles in the first instance, he received an official police caution. That, his parents hoped, would be the end of it. Efforts were made to ensure he did not mix with 'bad elements' and care was taken about what time he came in at night and where he was going when he went out. Nevertheless, four months later he was once again involved in a burglary and one of the boys from the school who had been involved in the previous incident was involved as well. This time he was not cautioned but was brought to court where the magistrate called him a 'juvenile delinquent', which of cause he now was by virtue of the offences he had committed.

Whether this would ever have taken place but for the imprisonment of his father and the consequent change in his peer group is a question which cannot be answered with certainty but in the opinion of the teacher there seemed to be a definite link which led to Peter's downfall. Throughout this saga the school played a completely passive role.[10]

Not infrequently, delinquent behaviour was reported by teachers as following in the wake of a father's imprisonment, but whether there is a causal relationship, or whether, given the family background, example and environment, to name just a few possibilities, the child's criminality was inevitable, is impossible to say. What can be said is that examples of children with previously good conduct displaying severe problems, including thieving, following their fathers' imprisonment were not infrequent.[11]

Links with social work agencies and with the probation service are vital if a school is to offer the maximum support to children of problem families particularly those with imprisoned fathers. Good liaison is frequently lacking, each agency dealing with its own priorities. Mistrust is often present. Ruth Clarke, writing from the standpoint of a head-teacher, called recently for more understanding between social workers and teachers: 'We have to understand the parameters of our responsibilities but be prepared at times to cross those boundaries with mutual understanding.'[12] The importance of Clarke's comments cannot be too strongly emphasised in relation to the children of imprisoned fathers. This is addressed in the final chapter.

The fact that children display widely differing responses when their father is imprisoned has already been commented on. It is particularly noticeable in the school setting. Whilst some are so distraught that they cease learning and in some cases refuse to attend school, others flourish when father is off the scene. Teachers reported some children being better dressed, despite the reduction in the family income. Others spoke of improved attendance and punctuality. In other cases no change was detected. Sometimes marked differences were apparent within the same family. In one case an older child progressed very well at school, gave no cause for concern and achieved several A levels. By contrast his younger brother was sullen, morose and unable to concentrate, traits which developed, according to the teacher, at the time father was first sent to prison.

For more than six hours a day, almost two hundred days a year, children are under the influence of their school. For those from disadvantaged environments and especially those where the father has prison experience, the influence and support of the school can be crucial. When one considers these two elements—the situation of these children and the unique position of teachers in relation to them—it becomes evident that the teaching profession has a major responsibility.

The health visitor: a fairy Godmother?

In the same way as the teacher is potentially of crucial importance to the schoolchild whose father is imprisoned, so too can the health visitor be vital to the well-being of the pre-school child of an imprisoned father. The reasons are similar: both have contact with most children, unlike, for instance, social workers and education welfare officers who work only with a selected proportion.[13] The teacher will have longer and more continuous dealings with a child but these seldom extend to the home and mother. The health visitor, however, will be in contact with both the young child and his mother, frequently at a time when the mother is vulnerable, for instance shortly after the birth of her child when the fact that the baby's father is in prison may be particularly traumatic.

A health visitor visits the home soon after the infant reaches the age of ten days and thereafter at varying key ages, depending on local policy, until the child commences full-time education. The health visitor is also likely to see the child and the mother at clinics and through other health service provisions and facilities.

The mother of a very young child faces considerable difficulties when the father is imprisoned, examples of which appear repeatedly in this book. Some of these women have no support from elsewhere. Whilst talking about the difficulties of visiting her husband in prison, a woman with a young baby added:

It was terrible those first few weeks. Sometimes I looked at the baby and felt I wanted to smash its face in because what he [the husband] did that landed him inside was for me and the kid . . . . One morning I felt right bad, I was expecting my Giro from the social and it hadn't come, it was pissing with rain and on top of that we hadn't any food in. Think I also felt bad because I hit the kid the night before; I'd opened the last tin of baby food and the little sod threw it all over me. Then there was this knock on the door see, and this woman was there. I thought she was some snoop from the social but she was a health visitor. You know about them? They're like a social worker and a doctor all rolled into one and they know all about babies. It was funny really, there was me feeling all uptight and guilty about hitting the kid and there was her asking all sorts of questions. But she didn't seem to be prying and I even told her I'd hit him without her even asking, I suppose she knew it really but somehow I felt she wanted to help and wouldn't just grass me up. She got me some food for him and said she'd come back the next day, and she did—she really did! Just like she said she would!! She came regularly after that. It was funny really, she was like some fairy godmother. I think she thought I was some sort of needy person what with my bloke being inside. She got me going to the clinic with the kid, I hadn't been before, hadn't got round to it somehow, well you know how it is. You know she really seemed to care what happened to me and the kid, no one had ever treated me like that before . . . . Must be wonderful to have a job like that. If it hadn't been for her I might of—well you know what I mean.[14]

Like the majority of teachers contacted in connection with the Leicester prisoners' children, health visitors were helpful and cooperative. They also formed the largest single group of professionals responding to the author's letters in professional journals inviting case histories and information relevant to the study of the children of imprisoned fathers. Three health visitors from different parts of the country also enclosed letters from prisoners' wives and a further three women with a partner in prison wrote saying they had been urged to do so by their health visitor.

The two three-month samples of men received into Leicester Prison produced 22 children belonging to nine families where the mother or guardian outside prison had given agreement for the health visitor to be interviewed. In several instances more than one health visitor was involved because of changes of staff. In addition, some of the health visitors interviewed had considerable knowledge of this problem in the area where they worked (or had previously worked); they were therefore able to comment extensively from their experiences.[15]

Although in theory all infants are seen by a health visitor, cases were discovered where this was not happening. Sometimes this was because the family concerned frequently and suddenly changed address and it was difficult to trace them. Another reason for some families being missed was the difficulty they found in getting on a doctor's list. Cases were described where a doctor had removed a woman from the list because of the problems she and her family had presented.[16] Uneducated, inarticulate patients are frequently unable to cope with such a situation, with the Family Practitioner Committee, or with the disinterest of a doctor. Similarly, some doctors may be unable to deal with these 'problem families', the unnecessary visits they are called out to make and the total culture clash. If children suffer as a result, once again it is the child of the prisoner, often in deprived circumstances, who is at the bottom of the 'pecking order'. The role of the health visitor is obviously crucial in these situations but in many parts of the country where they are attached to GP's surgeries, a family which keeps changing its GP has no regular health visitor either.

Another point relating to medical service is relevant here. Arber and Sawyer[17] have described the power of the doctor's receptionist with whom patients have to negotiate in order for the doctor to see themselves or their children. They describe the obstacles which are sometimes placed in the patient's way. In relation to single parent families Phillips observed, ' . . . it requires much energy, motivation and determination to ascertain, demand and receive one's full entitlements and rights. Many lone parents are too crushed and inarticulate to cope with bureaucratic blandishments. They may lack the energy, time and money to make long bus journeys, perhaps with their children, from offices to clinics to community centres, trying to get help from indifferent or ignorant officials.'[18] While it would be both wrong and unfair to brand all doctors' receptionists as 'dragons', the role of the health visitor in respect of those that are, and where a vulnerable family is not getting the service appropriate to its needs, can be important. Comments from some health visitors suggested that they usually know how patients are likely to be treated and where their own intervention might be appropriate.

Health visitors in poor districts tended to have a number of families where the father had prison experience. In many instances they listed a catalogue of problems and tragedy common to the same family: father in prison or about to go in; damaged child or loss of a child; drug, alcohol or solvent abuse; health, employment and money problems. To health visitors in such areas, as with probation officers and social workers, the pattern is familiar. Unfortunately, like teachers, health visitors were sometimes unaware that a father was in prison. Sometimes this was explainable by way of the complex or transient relationships within the family unit, in others because the woman did not wish to disclose the fact and explained her husband's absence by saying that he was working away, 'on an oil rig' and so on. When they did know, the level of liaison with probation officers and other relevant people was often non-existent. Seldom are health visitors informed of a father's imprisonment. The following case, described by a health visitor, is an example of a complete lack of communication on the part of a number of agencies:

> A husband and wife were both sent to prison. The downstairs doors and windows of their home were boarded up by the authorities to secure the house and reduce the likelihood of vandalism. Later that day the neighbours heard shouting, crying and banging. On investigation they discovered the distraught young child of the family, who had returned home from school, frantically trying to get in. No one had remembered her![19]

Many needy families with a father in prison receive considerable help and support from their health visitor. However, in a number of instances the workload of the health visitor is such that she is unable to offer the additional help necessary. With health visitors, as with teachers, there is often a clustering of problems (and indeed of prisoners' children) in certain districts; often there if not enough time available to properly advise the mother or to deal with problems which can affect the infant's destiny.

Neighbours: friend or foe?

Alan was about nine years old. His father had been sent to prison for a sexual assault on a small boy. Such was the level of local feeling, this being a particularly unpleasant case, that Alan's mother was insulted whenever she went out of the house. The windows of their home were broken by stones and other damage done to the front fence. At school Alan was branded the son of a sexual pervert and his life became a misery. One day, on his way home from school, he was set upon in the street by adult neighbours. He was pushed to the ground and his face rubbed in dog's excrement.

This case, known personally to the author, is an extreme example but shows the impact which a man's offence can have on his child. It is horrific because it demonstrates that although local adults were revolted by the man's crime, their desire for retribution caused them to behave in a manner which was no less reprehensible. Their child victim was as innocent as the child victim they sought to avenge. One wonders if those men and women responsible feel guilt or shame; what do others in the street, who knew about the incident but did not take part, now feel in their hearts? Most of all, one wonders what this event did to Alan, coming as it did on top of the publicity given to his father's case and his father being labelled a 'fiend' and a 'sexual pervert'.

Unpleasant, aggressive behaviour of neighbours towards the family of prisoners is not uncommon and has been touched on earlier.[20] However, it has also been observed that neighbours will sometimes go to ‹considerable lengths to offer help. When asked about sources of support, mothers in the Leicester samples gave the following information:

Table 4   *Sources of support to mothers in Leicester Sample*

neighbours	29%
friends	38%
family	52%
probation officers ⎫ social workers | health visitors ⎬ 38% other professionals | and volunteers ⎭	
no support	14%

As the figures suggest, many of the women said they had support from several sources. It was also evident that many of the 'friends' were also neighbours; the true figure for neighbours is probably nearer to 50 per cent. As a prisoner's cohabitee put it, 'You get help from those neighbours who are friends'. It is important to bear in mind that the numbers concerned are small; nevertheless, correspondents from elsewhere in the country also supported the view that neighbours do provide considerable support in many instances, especially where the neighbourhood is well-established. A sizeable number had support only from statutory agencies or voluntary bodies. The need of a young woman with children and whose man is in prison to have someone to turn to cannot be stressed too strongly. The fact that 14 per cent felt they had no support from anyone is cause for concern.

In some highly delinquent areas imprisonment is such a common occurrence that informal arrangements of neighbourliness have developed to assist women whose men are sent down. Whilst such developments undoubtedly help the women concerned (and so far as material standards are concerned, the children too), one is forced to question what such an acceptance of the normality of imprisonment of men does to the developing morality of their children. Some probation officers and health visitors described outstanding examples of neighbourliness in which children were taken into another family for quite lengthy periods. Also long-term help was provided in the form of shopping, taking to school and other duties. Interviews and correspondence with residential care staff, however, were a reminder of just how frequently a family is unable to cope when the man is sent to prison and the repercussions on the children when they are put into 'care'.[21]

The response of neighbours, although often a factor of the social class of the district, seems very much to depend on the extent of existing relationships. People who were unpopular to begin with were, not surprisingly, those who suffered most. The scapegoated child was bullied more and the 'slut down the road' became more of a slut in the eyes of those who disliked her before her man was imprisoned. This, however, was not always the case and examples were brought to notice where a family which had previously experienced no problems with the neighbours became a target for attack following the man's imprisonment. Some families were driven out of their homes; lighted rags and paper were pushed through the letterbox and missiles thrown at the windows.[22]

Once again a picture of great variation was described, including, frequently, a real concern for the child by neighbours. This concern seems not to be shared by society as a whole, despite a caring, sentimental or emotional response to babies and children in some other forums.[23]

Other important people

In this chapter teachers, health visitors and neighbours have already been singled out as being of particular significance to children of imprisoned fathers. It could, of course, be argued that these groups of people or the services they provide are important to most children. While this is certainly so, the special position of the prisoner's child, frequently multi-deprived, stigmatised and at the bottom of the 'pecking order' makes the contribution of these groups all the more important. In the absence of their attention the child may be left with no support at all. Teachers and health visitors come into contact with the children of imprisoned fathers whether or not they choose to; neighbours are always close by. Other people who become involved with the child do so as a result of a selective administrative process, for instance probation officers, education welfare officers and social workers, or else they have made a personal decision to help. As a result, prisoners' children in different parts of the country are in receipt of variable attention from a widely disparate group of professionals, voluntary workers, friends and relatives—or are in receipt of no help at all. It is largely a matter of chance.

Grandparents, distant relatives and new 'uncles' acquired by mother for the duration of her husband's incarceration, were found sometimes to be very loving and supportive of the child. Schoolfriends and the parents of schoolfriends were also found to be attentive in some instances, notwithstanding the example to the contrary earlier in this chapter. Where a probation officer or social worker is involved with the family there may be an introduction to other agencies or voluntary organisations which provide advice and material help to the mother.

The list of those who may be important persons to the prisoner's child is endless. It is not the purpose of this chapter to list them but merely to draw attention to the fact that the availability of help to the children of an imprisoned father is a matter of chance.

One other group of significant importance to some prisoners' children must be mentioned; the staff of residential children's homes. It is not known how many children go into residential care directly or indirectly as a result of their father being sent to prison. It was not possible to discover that figure from this research. What is known from interviews with residential care staff is that it happens, and even the small Leicester samples disclosed some cases.[24]

Notes

1 The child of the prisoner is not alone in this respect. Divorce, desertion and bereavement all inflict their toll. There are, however, important differences with regard to imprisonment. The effect of stigma was raised earlier, in Chapters 1 and 2; problems peculiar to the wives and cohabitees of prisoners which rebound on the children were discussed in Chapters 3 and 4.

2 This has been referred to on several occasions but see especially Wilson, H. (1974) and Phillips, K. (1985).

3 The mechanism of this process is discussed in Chapter 7.

4 See Chapter 1 regarding the socio-economic grouping of prisoners' families.

5 See Chapter 4, 'What Children Are Told'.

6 The number of children whose fathers are imprisoned is considered in Chapter 6.

7 Headteachers were given a letter from the child's mother giving her consent to information being divulged; confidentiality in respect of identification was promised. The ethical problems associated with assuming the mother's right to make such decisions whilst the father is in prison were touched on in Chapter 1.

8 Shaw, R.G. 'Schools and Prisoners' Children'—paper in the course of preparation.

9 See for example Drake (1981) and Riley and Lund (1984).

10 Interview with teacher.

11 For an example of deterioration in two brothers of previously good experience following their father being remanded in custody see Knight (1984) quoted in Chapter 2.

12 Clarke, R. (1985).

13 This does not indicate that social workers are insensitive to the needs of children of imprisoned fathers. However, their clients are referred to them from elsewhere or else refer themselves. They do not automatically include all prisoners' families and in practice include very few. There is also a tendency for social services departments to view these people as the responsibility of the probation service. This is discussed further in Chapter 7.

14 Interview with a prisoner's wife.
15 A more detailed account of the findings of this study and of further work will be found in Shaw, R.G. 'Health Visitors and Prisoners' Children'—paper in course of preparation.
16 Source: probation officers, volunteer workers, health visitors, and prisoners' wives from different parts of the country.
17 Arber and Sawyer (1985).
18 Phillips, K. (1985).
19 Interview with health visitor. Consider also the cases described in Chapter 2 and Chapter 4, 'The Orphans of Justice'.
20 See Chapter 3, 'The Problems of the Mother'.
21 See Chapter 4.
22 Interviews with prisoners' wives.
23 See Chapter 1.
24 See also Chapters 1, 4 and 6.

6

Child Abuse on a Massive Scale

'Crime is the end point of a continuum of disorder. It is not separate
from other forms of aggravation and breakdown. It is the rundown
council estate whose music blares out of windows early in the morning;
it is the graffiti on the walls; it is aggression in the shops . . . it is streets
you dare not walk down at night, it is always being careful, it is a symbol
of a world falling apart. It is lack of respect for humanity and for
fundamental human decency. Crime is the tip of the iceberg. It is a real
problem in itself but it is also a symbol of a far greater problem; and the
weak suffer most'—Lea and Young (1984). The authors might also have
added, 'and the weakest of the weak are the children of imprisoned
criminals'.

The pain and harm inflicted unintentionally on children by the
sentencer of their father could be described as 'institutionalised child
abuse'. If the samples are at all characteristic of prison receptions
nationally, the total number of children whose fathers are imprisoned in
any one year would be very great. Table 5 shows the age range of the two
Leicester samples alongside national receptions. Direct comparison is
not possible because the samples include fine defaulters and exclude
men sentenced to more than six months. Official figures do not indicate

Table 5 *Age range of men over 21 as percentage of receptions*

| Age | Sentences of up to six months including fine defaulters | | All sentences and remands but excluding fine defaulters National figures, England and Wales. One year[1] |
| | Sample A n=202 | Sample B n=213 | |
	%	%	%
21–24	33	35	35
25–29	19	16	23
30–39	31	25	25
40–49	11	17	11
50–59	5	5	4
60 and over	1	1	1

The actual number of separate individuals received into Prison Department
Establishments in England and Wales in a year is not known and cannot be
calculated by adding together the different groups identified.

the ages of men received into prison in default of payment of fines, maintenance or rates.

The actual number of separate individuals received into Prison Department Establishments in England and Wales in a year is not known and cannot be calculated by adding together the different groups identified in tables in the *Prison Statistics*.[2] There are several reasons for this, the most significant being that a number of people are received into prison more than once in any one year. Sometimes they are given a new prison number, sometimes not. Taking these factors into consideration, together with what is known from the Leicester samples, one is able to suggest that about 75,000 separate adult males were received into prison in England and Wales in 1984.

The two Leicester samples are not markedly different from national receptions in terms of age. If their production of children is similar, then on the basis that 415 prisoners are known to have produced more than 584 children (the figure does not include pregnancies or the high proportion of 'no answers' to the question about children elsewhere), 75,000 adult receptions might produce more than 100,000 children in England and Wales alone.[3] This figure would be swollen by offspring of the under twenty-one-year-olds—a not inconsiderable number judging from the observations of prison chaplains and health visitors.

Of sample A, 31 per cent and 33 per cent of sample B had not been in prison before. This suggests that the number of children in England and Wales whose father is imprisoned during their childhood could be quite high. The prevalence of convictions for non-motoring offences is very high for males (Farrington,[4] Home Office[5]). The proportion of the male population which is composed of former inmates of penal institutions or even just adult Prison Department Establishments, is not known, so a reliable statistic in regard to their children is even harder to acquire. However, on the basis of the figures referred to here, the number must be in excess of half a million children whose father is imprisoned during their childhood. This represents more than five per cent of the population of approximately ten million children under 16.[6]

It must be emphasised that some of the comparisons and extrapolations made in this paper are necessarily tentative, simply because the necessary data is not available. However, throughout, a conservative interpretation of the figures has been taken and the total arrived at is probably a considerable understatement of the actual number; the true figure may be nearer ten per cent.[7] It may not yet be possible to demonstrate the exact number of children involved, but what we can say with certainty is that the number is very large.

Many children have no contact with their natural father so his imprisonment is an irrelevance so far as they are concerned. Even in these cases there may be indirect effects such as the cessation of maintenance payments in the few cases where the father was working and an order was in force. For many more, he is a parent, and his imprisonment is a significant event. Quite apart from letters from correspondents and interviews elsewhere in the country, the Leicester samples alone produced a number of cases which gave rise to concern. Two children of a single-parent father were taken into care and separated when their father was imprisoned. A mother who was unable to cope alone with her handicapped son was left alone when her husband was imprisoned for not paying a fine imposed for using a television set without a licence. Rent money in one man's possession was taken from him to offset unpaid fines but he was imprisoned for the outstanding amount, leaving his wife to try and resolve the crisis. Numerous men imprisoned for non-payment of fines imposed for road traffic offences left pregnant or sick wives or handicapped children; some had never been in prison before. One man was imprisoned for motoring offences leaving his partially blind and epileptic daughter in the care of his pregnant, epileptic wife.

Again it should be emphasised that these cases were drawn only from the 415 men in the two Leicester samples. These samples consisted of men sentenced to less than six months, and represented only two three-month periods in one prison. The catchment area of the prison is far from being one of the more deprived areas of the country. The national picture, therefore, must be of concern to all thinking men and women, whatever their political views or attitudes to crime and punishment. The social situation of the mother impinges on the child of the prisoner and once more Phillips' comments about crushed, inarticulate lone parents, quoted earlier, are brought to mind.[8]

The child's right to protection is enshrined in principles of the United Nations' 'Declaration of the Rights of the Child, 1959'. Amnesty International has categorised separation as a form of child abuse. Both are flouted in respect of the children of imprisoned fathers. In an effort to offer some explanation one is forced to enquire into politics—both politics and Politics—the politics of injustice.

Notes

1 *Prison Statistics, England and Wales* (1984).
2 *Prison Statistics* op. cit.
3 See Chapter 1.
4 Farrington, D. (1981).
5 Home Office (1985).
6 Central Statistical Office (1985) *Annual Abstract of Statistics.*
7 The number of children concerned is discussed in more detail in Shaw, R.G. (1986) 'The Prevalence of Children of Imprisoned Fathers'.
8 Phillips, K. (1985).

7

The Politics of Injustice

> Punishment is neither a simple consequence of crime, nor the reverse side of crime, nor a mere means which is determined by the end to be achieved. Punishment must be understood as a social phenomenon freed from both its juristic concept and its social ends—Rusche and Kirchheimer (1938).

The plight of children entangled in what Davis describes as 'the web of punishment meted out to their fathers',[1] is inextricably entwined with the politics of criminal justice and the long-demonstrated need of society for retribution for the crime rather than the reparation of its consequences. Until recently the children of prisoners were not the only victims of crime and criminal justice to be ignored by the system. Actual victims of crime received little recognition or help, their only role being to report an offence and then, in the event of the accused pleading not guilty, to be called to court as a witness and cross-examined. However, matters improved with the introduction of the Criminal Injuries Compensation Board and increased pressure on courts to use their powers to make compensation orders. There was also a growing interest in reparation and the development of victim support schemes. Nevertheless, the National Association of Victim Support Schemes is starved of the funds necessary to ensure nationwide standards and support for its volunteer workers. Until 1985, NAVSS had only one professional member of staff. Some local victim support schemes received a grant from the DHSS under the 'Opportunities for Volunteering' initiative, some others had finance from the Manpower Services Commission or an urban aid programme but in the main, victim support is almost entirely dependent on voluntary effort and cash from charities. Meanwhile, government extols the virtues of victim support. Given this record with regards to actual victims of crime, what hope is there for the hidden victims, namely the children of offenders? These youngsters are victims not only of their fathers' criminality but also of the system which dispenses 'justice'.

By contrast to the meagre amount of money spent on behalf of victims of crime and the children of prisoners, the State apportions vast sums to the punishment of the offender. In a written parliamentary answer in 1985, David Mellor stated, 'Total estimated Central Government expenditure on law and order services in England and Wales during the current financial year will be one thousand and eighty-seven million pounds. The Department is making a grant to the National Association of Victim Support Schemes of up to one hundred and twenty thousand pounds, which represents approximately 0.01 per cent of this total: and some thirty-seven million pounds (or 3.4 per cent) will be spent on compensating victims through the Criminal Injuries Compensation Scheme.'[2] The huge prison component in the law and order budget might be justified if it was spent on keeping dangerous men out of circulation. However, it is not. As has already been observed, a quarter of prison receptions in England and Wales are of men who have been committed for non-payment of a fine, frequently for a road traffic offence. Fifty per cent of the remainder sentenced by the courts for criminal and other offences are given no more than six months'.[3] These short sentences are obviously not aimed at the protection of the public yet they are passed by the courts in the absence of evidence to suggest that prison either reforms or deters.[4] Many times during the course of the research described in this book, wives of prisoners explained with bitterness that they and their children—not their husbands—were 'serving the sentence'. It was interesting to note that some inmates also recognised this; their basic needs of food, warmth, clothing and shelter were adequately met by the prison, which also provided the additional benefit of sheltering them from the pressures and responsibilities of the outside world in which their families still had to exist.

The literature on the criminal justice and penal systems is awash with books and articles on juvenile justice, the rights of children and arguments about 'the best interests of the child'.[5] A child's rights and interests are, it seems, seriously considered when it is a juvenile offender, but not at all when it is the offspring of an adult criminal. Let us not forget, however, as Morris and her colleagues have cryptically observed, 'What is in the child's "best interests" frequently conforms with social and political expediency'.[6] Feaver,[7] in his historical review of the use and development of Unruly Certificates gives a vivid insight into the way in which cruelty to children was condoned because it was expedient so to do. Outside the criminal justice system, politicians, academics and journalists, whether inspired by goodly intent or other motives, write about the effects of different aspects of law, housing policy, education and health services on children. The impact of poor accommodation, inadequate play facilities and cuts in educational provision are constantly brought to the attention of the public. One hundred thousand children in England and Wales are annually affected by the loss of their father into prison but no one has taken up their cause. Why is this? Parliamentary silence can perhaps be explained by the fact that public uninterest means there are no votes in this issue. If, in a democracy, the work of parliament reflects the will of the people, democracy is bought at a high price: a hundred thousand children a year cannot be judged inexpensive by any standards, especially by a country which views itself as being among the most just and civilised nations on earth. In pursuance of its efforts to reduce public expenditure, Government talks of the need to keep offenders out of prison wherever possible. Both the Green Paper on *Intermittent Custody* and the Home Office paper on *Criminal Justice*[8] made mention of families to support the argument for alternatives to imprisonment. However, a high proportion of men received into prison do not have families or else are already parted from them.

Official reports and enquiries of recent years which have purported to address the subject of prisons and imprisonment have not had in their remit the unintended consequences of a man's imprisonment on his children, or else they have paid scant attention to it.[9] The Home Office's working paper *Criminal Justice*[10] ignores the subject altogether. It is as if government is prepared to talk about offenders' families in order to try to persuade courts to use prison sparingly, but once a man is committed to custody his family is somehow spirited away. The Home Office 'Statement of National Objectives and Priorities for the Probation Service in England and Wales' lays down priorities which do not include prisoners' children.[11] Social Services Departments, however, are usually quick to view any referral of a prisoner's family as the proper responsibility of the local probation service.

The tendency of social welfare organisations to move in a direction of social control was found to be a cause of concern to many professionals. Probation officers concerned about the Home Office Statement of Objectives and Priorities for the Service questioned who would now be responsible for helping those minor offenders who come before the courts in need of advice, assistance and befriending. The answer, they said, was 'No one'. Health visitors in one area had received an instruction from their management that they were to strip children they visited to guard against child abuse. Some argued that this type of policing was counter-productive; even if handled tactfully it could antagonise mothers of 'problem families'—the very ones where it was important to establish a sound relationship. All the Health Authority instruction did do was to safeguard management, to make it appear that management was managing, and to provide a ready-made scapegoat in the case of an abused child which the health visitor had not undressed.[12]

For too long the prison service has been allowed to treat the inmate's child as an irrelevance. The restrictive attitudes of the Prison Officers Association have not been challenged, neither has the absolute silence on the subject from the Prison Department. Whilst many prison officers are undoubtedly considerate, humane and professional in their dealings with the families of inmates, a minority are not. When members of that minority are undertaking tasks which give them great power over other people, such as being in charge of the prison gate, they are able to turn visitors away for very trivial reasons, such as loss of a visiting order, even though it would be possible to verify if one had been issued and was valid. Such actions on the part of officers who may have worked long hours on repetitive tasks are perhaps understandable—but should they be ignored or condoned? If the interests of children were seriously taken into consideration by the system no visitor would be turned away without referral to a higher authority such as an Assistant Governor. The omens for the future are even worse. A prison chaplain wrote, 'Chaplains have been discouraged from being over-involved with families outside prison'.[13] Another stated, 'It is prison department policy that we confine our activities to the inmates within the establishment.'[14] NACRO in its April 1986 *Digest* stated, 'The right of remand prisoners to daily visits is to be curtailed, according to a Home Office Circular sent to all prisons in England and Wales. It says that the Home Secretary has agreed that in view of the current pressures caused by the increase in the unconvicted population on many local prisons and remand centres, governors may seek permission from regional directors to vary the pattern of visits, which allows prisoners a minimum of six fifteen-minute visits a week.'[15] This is a further example of the 'operational needs' of a prison taking priority over the rights of children to see their fathers.

Such moves as are made on behalf of prisoners' children come about largely as a result of efforts from the voluntary sector, frequently assisted by probation officers who may or may not be involved at the behest of their management. Sometimes probation officers will be acting as volunteers themselves and helping voluntary bodies in their own time. Some organisations are independent groups in their own right, such as the Leicester Prison Visits Centre which is concerned solely with prisoners' families.[16] In other cases a Prison Visits or Family Centre may be a facility operated by a larger group.[17] Sometimes an element of public funding is involved, such as a capital grant towards the purchase of premises or an MSC post to pay for a volunteer coordinator, but in the main the support from official channels is far too small given the scale of the problem.

Much is written and spoken about the adverse effects of imprisonment on inmates, largely by those who seek to criticise the penal system or reduce the use of imprisonment or the length of sentences. However, have all these oft-quoted adverse effects on a prisoner been adequately demonstrated?[18] It is interesting that so many penal reform groups have concentrated their efforts on the supposed destructive impact of incarceration on the inmate whilst paying so little attention to the prisoner's child, who is wholly innocent of any crime. Even on the simplest level, that of unhappiness and confusion, the unintended punishment meted out on many children by the sentencer of their father is apparent even to the casual observer. More serious responses to their father's sentence have been described elsewhere in this book. Where particular pain and suffering is endured by a child, can our society continue to describe it as 'an unfortunate consequence of imprisonment' and put it out of mind?

Many cases were described to the researcher in which the pain suffered by the child as a result of the father's imprisonment far exceeded that which was caused to the original victim of the offence.

It is easy to criticise the criminal justice and the penal systems on a great number of points: the inequality of justice, disparity in sentencing and the enormous cost to name but a few. However, to effect some change in its operation is a very different matter. Like any large organisation the criminal justice system has its own inertia. It is a vast multi-million pound industry; it provides jobs for many tens of thousands, fortunes for a few and a respected, priviliged position for many. Yet almost all it does in reality is endeavour to identify the culprit of a crime and then punish that person. It is hoped that in so doing it will appease public opinion, deter would-be offenders and define boundaries of acceptable behaviour but it does little else and whether it achieves even these simple objectives is doubtful. The system is centred on the offender; the victim of the crime has scant recognition, the family of the offender that the system punishes, none. This is all too apparent in the Home Secretary's speech quoted in *Criminal Justice*.[19]

There is considerable vested interest in the criminal justice system remaining as it is; there are few powerful lobies on behalf of the victims of crime and none on behalf of prisoners' children. The behaviour of government and populace alike towards this problem is an indictment of a civilised society; the matter has been totally ignored. Has it been ignored because, as Davis observed, any recognition of the plight of children of prisoners strikes at the very roots of the established system of criminal justice, which is based on the concept of individual punishment for individual law-breaking and the notions of 'justice', 'innocence' and 'guilt'?[20] The whole basis of justice and punishment collapses when one repeatedly identifies children of prisoners who suffer more as a result of their father's sentence than did the original victim of the offence. The problem of children of imprisoned fathers has been 'swept under the carpet' but unlike many problems this one will not go away: rather the reverse, in time. One hundred thousand children a year are not going to disappear; they are growing older every day, growing up subject to multiple disadvantage and pain, soon to be adolescents and then young adults. We should all know what that means, not only to them but also to the community of which they are members.

Serious consideration of the issues raised by the plight of so many children whose fathers are imprisoned calls into question not only the major planks on which the justice system is founded but also the individual strands of that system and the way in which it is used.

As an example one can consider the effect of unemployment on sentencing practice. Sentencers are urged, by probation officers and others, to bear in mind the employment situation and think seriously of the implications before sending a man to prison, to be released into unemployment. If such consideration is given it introduces yet another variable into the sentence decision-making process, creates further injustice (since many men are unemployed through no fault of their own), and amplifies the disadvantage of the families of unemployed offenders. Only a tiny proportion of the Leicester prison reception sample were employed prior to being imprisoned. Box observed that unemployed men are more likely to be given immediate prison sentences and the unemployed also represent a high proportion of imprisoned fine defaulters.[21] Unemployment has few beneficial effects but one which it does appear to have is to provide the environment in which some fathers can become more involved in the care and upbringing of their infants. This is particularly advantageous where the woman is a less than competent mother and where the man, otherwise the provider, seeks an alternative role in the family. The impact of his imprisonment on the delicate dynamics of such a situation can be dramatic; health visitors and some other correspondents highlighted instances of families, who had previously coped adequately, collapsing or requiring considerable input from health, social and other welfare agencies following imprisonment of the father, even for a very short period.[22]

Because the majority of the families in the sample, and those reported on by correspondents, tended to have complex family situations, were educationally disadvantaged and resided in poor areas, the imprisonment of a father becomes just one further wound in a child whose life prospects are already far below average. Nevertheless, many children do learn to survive. They develop a response which seems to insulate them from pain. What this does to their ability to make meaningful relationships in later life is another matter and an area worthy of research.

This study identified three cases in the Leicester sample and many others brought to attention by the staff of residential children's homes, where children had been taken into care following the imprisonment of their father. Sometimes this was because the man was a single parent, or because the mother was unable to cope alone or was judged so by the social services. There were instances where the home circumstances had been so bad in terms of parenting that the child stood to benefit from the move but generally such a state of affairs was considered deplorable. In many of these cases there had been no social inquiry report prior to the sentence.

In much the same way that the location and characteristics of a prison can amplify the punishment inflicted on an offender's wife and children, so too can individual family factors act as stressors and heighten feelings of helplessness. Illiteracy in the mother, inability to speak English, very low intelligence and an absence of social skills become serious matters if the able parent is taken away. However, probably the most difficult problem that a mother has to face when her husband is imprisoned is that of continuing to cope with a seriously sick, or physically or mentally handicapped child. The incidence of such situations was found to be alarmingly high.

'The United Kingdom imprisons more people, both in absolute numbers and in proportion to its population, than other comparable nations in Western Europe.'[23] It follows, therefore, that the number of its children who suffer the unintended consequences of their fathers' incarceration is similarly greater.

The politics of criminal justice coupled with the need for retribution renders the plight of the prisoner's child one which most strands of public opinion have chosen to leave alone. This has permitted legislators, policy-makers and criminal justice decision-makers to ignore it. If such a state of affairs continues it will be because society allows it to be so; a demonstration that the veneer of civilisation is very thin indeed. Walker has observed, 'In a non-sadistic culture the deliberate infliction of death, pain or harm is seen as requiring a very strong justification if it is not to be condemned.'[24] Since it is manifestly clear that much pain and harm is inflicted on the children of prisoners, albeit unintentionally, society is faced with a moral dilemma of considerable proportions. Is it possible that the most highly developed species on earth can continue to take no interest in such a large group of its own young? Can we continue not to meet our responsibilities?

Notes

1 Davis L. (1983).
2 Hansard (1985). But spending on the entire criminal justice system is far greater; £4½ billion in 1986, *Criminal Justice* (revised edition), 1986.
3 Home Office (1985) *Prison Statistics England and Wales 1984*.
4 For a brief comment on the relationship between punishment and reparation see Evans (1986).
5 For instance see Freeman (1983), Morris, A. (1978), Morris *et al.* (1980) and the extensive bibliography in the latter covering this subject.
6 Morris op. cit.
7 Feaver (1985).
8 Home Office (1984) *Intermittent Custody*, Home Office (1984) *Criminal Justice*.
9 Examples of this are May Report (1979): Report of the Long Term Review Committee (1985); and Annual Reports of the Prison Department.
10 *Criminal Justice* op. cit.
11 Home Office (1984) Probation Service in England and Wales: Statement of National Objectives and Priorities.
12 Personal correspondence.
13 Personal correspondence.
14 Personal correspondence.
15 NACRO *Digest* April (1986).
16 A Charitable Trust; see Appendix.
17 For instance, the Families Outside Project in Glasgow which is associated with the Scottish Council for Civil Liberties. Also the scheme at Cromlin

Road which is run by Save The Children. There are numerous other examples.

18 In this respect see Coker and Martin (1985).
19 Home Office (1984) *Criminal Justice* op. cit.
20 Davis op. cit.
21 Box, S. (1986).
22 See Chapter 4, 'The Orphans of Justice'.
23 NACRO briefing August (1985).
24 Walker, N. (1979). See also Bartle, R. (1986).

8

Meeting Our Responsibility

It will be evident from the preceding pages that what happens to the children of imprisoned fathers and whether or not help is available is largely a matter of chance. Yet almost a quarter of a century ago, Friedman and Esselstyn, commenting on their own research findings observed:

> Provision for special attention to children at the time of their fathers' confinement should be part of general social service practice everywhere. It should be well-planned, effective and part of standard operating procedures. It should not be left to chance or the unusual incident.[1]

Such provision is still left to chance and to 'unusual incident'. For matters to be made different requires a change in attitudes and an acceptance of responsibility for their part in the process by people inside and outside the criminal justice system. The previous chapter described some of the pressures and vested interests which resist change and seek to maintain the *status quo*. In this final part we address what might be done to improve the lot of prisoners' children and reduce the element of chance in responding to their needs—without major changes in legislation and largely within current financial constraints.

Some will perhaps argue that no significant improvement is likely to be made without a major overhaul of the entire justice system and the principles upon which it is based; that argument will be addressed very briefly later. The point made here is that much of the misery suffered by these children is avoidable—provided that those adults who come into contact with them, and those who administer and staff the criminal justice and penal systems accept some responsibility and act. Additionally, political will must be engendered by the public voicing its concern.

The following suggestions are made in response to issues which arose in previous chapters. They are not exhaustive and readers will certainly have their own ideas about what should be done. Indeed, the main purpose of this book is to invite consideration of the issues and public debate on the subject.

Willingness on the part of the prison authorities and the POA could achieve much. This especially applies to a recognition of the priority which should be given to visits, both their frequency and the conditions under which they take place. In other words, visits should be seen as part of the right of the *child* to maintain a meaningful relationship with his father. It is appreciated that this raises issues about the location of prisoners and of ensuring that those without children are not treated unfairly. But if the prison service is to accept responsibility for its part in respect of these tens of thousands of children, these difficulties must be overcome. Many countries have far better visiting arrangements than those in the United Kingdom,[2] and better home-leave facilities too.[3] There is no justification for Britain having such an inferior, archaic system, dismissive of children's needs. Strong family communication should be a priority of the prison system, and not just dealt with in a glib phrase in prison service literature.[4] Quite apart from the welfare of children there may be other advantages, such as improved atmosphere in the prison and lower reconviction rates.[5]

Even men with very strong family ties may need counselling or at least someone to listen, as may their family outside. The agonising of a prisoner in respect of his children is clear from the following passage:

> At first I did not want my wife to bring my three children to visit me. To me it represented everything I had been taught not to do, and everything I have tried to teach my children not to do. Yet here I was and still am in the very situation I was always preaching about. I at first thought I would be given bail and could lie to my children about the misunderstanding that was taking place. As the weeks went by and I realised that there was not to be any bail for me, I wanted to see my children very much. I still thought then that I would tell them less than the truth, in order, or so I thought, to keep their love and respect for me. I have long since realised that in order to keep my self respect and those nearest and dearest to me that nothing but open frankness would do.
>
> As for my children's views of their father being in prison, I get the feeling that the love bond is still very strong between us and that is also reflected in the letters I get from them. They realise that I have done something wrong and am being punished for it. That one day it will end and I'll be able to go back home to them.[6]

How prisoners' families are treated and the priority afforded visits raises issues about the training and accountability of prison staff, responsibilities of Boards of Visitors and the importance of the role of probation officers in prisons. The fostering of good, meaningful contact between a man and his family should be part of good through-care practice. Nevertheless, it would be wrong to assume that even the most concerned prison staff can assess the needs of a man's family by interviewing him in the prison. Both the Leicester samples and correspondence from elsewhere pointed to this fact and how the real problems faced by the woman and her children were quite different from what her husband in prison indicated. This point cannot be made too strongly.[7] In order to establish the needs of the family, the home must be visited.[8] It is the woman who has to cope outside and hers should be the right to accept or decline any offer of help. The man in prison, although one hopes in full agreement, should have no right of veto. The experience of Leicester Prison Visits Centre Trust was that most women welcome a visit and that volunteers can undertake this task very well, when necessary linking families with other agencies.

The matter of what and how children are told is one of the most important issues over which parents have some control.[9] It is important to bear in mind, as Huxley-Robinson explained in connection with the bereaved child, that ' . . . parental attitudes are usually dictated by their own personal needs, rather than by any realistic appreciation of the needs of the children.'[10] There is an urgent need for adequate advice and counselling for all mothers faced with this dilemma. It is important for mothers to be helped to think through the implications of what they tell their children and to consider the possibility of the children finding out from elsewhere. They have to realise that being forced to deny the truth for ever and to live with the fear that it might one day come to light might well damage the child's relationship with his parents. Advice might extend beyond what exactly the child should be told to what responses might be expected, and how to deal with them. Morris recognised this need twenty years ago, and also the 'small but important move towards using volunteer workers to visit the wives of men in prison.'[11] However, she saw some hazards in this, commenting, ' . . . Nor are such volunteers trained to handle the usually quite serious emotional problems these children present, often in the form of psychosomatic symptoms.'[12] It is important here to make the point that the Leicester Prison Visits Centre home-visiting scheme showed clearly that volunteers can do much to enable the woman to cope better with her children. Even though the seriousness of some of the problems, as seen by Morris, should not be overlooked, much can be achieved by non-professionals, adequately supported and given a little training. Only on a few occasions did volunteers find it necessary to refer to other agencies. Of course it is impossible to say how many hidden problems were missed but what can be said is that in the absence of the volunteer's visit many of these families would have had no help or advice at all.

There is every reason to encourage a massive extention in the use of volunteers to support prisoners' families. Some probation services already give active cooperation and advice to voluntary bodies working in this area, so also do other organisations.[13] Recently, the wife of a prisoner formed an organisation to help families: HALOW—Help and Advice Line for Prisoners' Wives.[14] This is staffed entirely by wives of prisoners and is aiming to develop branches throughout the country to meet what it sees as a massive demand. In 1986 a book was published written by a man who was serving a prison sentence at the time, which gave advice to families and friends of men in prison. This contains a considerable amount of useful information.[15] The work of the voluntary sector is growing but is uncoordinated and still only able to touch the 'tip of the iceberg'.[16]

It was clear from this study that people who might be expected to attend to the needs of these children were frequently prevented from doing so by a lack of information or through being unaware of the situation: teachers, health visitors and social workers in particular, and also probation officers in respect of fine defaulters. Yet again one is reminded of the point made by Morris in 1967, 'Where children are of school age the problem might be less acute if teachers were given more information about the child's background, and in particular the fact that the father is in prison.'[17].The question of whether professionals like teachers should be given this information, other than by the family, is probably the most sensitive one to be grappled with in respect of improving provision for these children. It has to be addressed and debated thoroughly if teachers and others are to be able to develop a system whereby they can offer the maximum support to this grossly disadvantaged group. Morris's contention that 'The need for these children to receive help and understanding at such a critical time should outweigh the dangers of confidential information being misused'[18] deserves at least to be discussed and tested. It should not be dismissed solely on grounds of an ideological belief about confidentiality; but neither should it be introduced lightly or inadvisedly.

A prison chaplain suggested, ' . . . it would be helpful if probation officers who are involved in cases where court reports are required were to try to help parents to handle the question of their children's involvement.'[19] Many readers of this book may be amazed that this is not routine in cases where the man is likely to be sent to prison. Probation officers are only involved with a proportion of men who are incarcerated but when they are, they constitute a link with the family which can allow the needs of any children to be considered. This does not necessarily involve the active use of scarce probation officer time; sometimes a volunteer worker is allocated to that family and subsequent referral to another agency is made only if the circumstances justify it. This should be routine.

Much can be done within the current system. However, in the long term we may discover that significant reduction in the distress unintentionally meted out by the courts to tens of thousands of children every year can only be resolved by a serious reappraisal of the objectives of the criminal justice system and the methods it employs. Currently the bulk of the enormous criminal justice budget is spent on catching, convicting and punishing the offender; victims of crime receive only a pittance, the children of prisoners who are inextricably entangled in the events, even less. In terms of resource allocation we are nowhere near the right balance. Help, assistance, care and support for prisoners' children occur mainly by change or favour. A teacher in an area of high crime and victimisation put his point strongly, saying, ' ... for allowing this situation to develop where these kids [of prisoners] get no help at all while millions are spent on prisons, every adult stands indicted'.[20] Will we continue to stand indicted? A prisoner's wife at a visits centre said, in relation to this study, 'Even if you do show what is happening to these kids, nothing will happen. Influential people will do nothing because there is nothing in it for them. They will either say it isn't true or they will ignore it'.[21] Similar comments were made by other people, including some occupying very senior positions in the criminal justice system.

Even from this small study, with all its limitations, it is abundantly clear that the scale of the problem and the degree of neglect are enormous. Similarly it will also become clear whether steps are to be taken to remedy it or whether the cynicism voiced by some is justified. There is a need for extensive research into the long-term effects of fathers' imprisonment on children; an official enquiry into how distress can be reduced, how volunteer resources can be coordinated and the role of statutory agencies, and informed public debate to which this book is just one small contribution. In the absence of serious attention to this issue we shall not meet our responsibility to these tens of thousands of children and as the teacher said, we will 'stand indicted'. More than that, in view of the clear evidence, we will stand convicted.

Notes

1 Friedman and Esselstyn (1965).
2 NACRO (1985) 'Visits to Prisoners'.
3 NACRO (1985) 'Home Leave'.
4 Prison Standing Order Number 5 states, 'It is one of the roles of the prison service to ensure that the socially harmful effects of an inmate's removal from normal life are so far as possible minimised and that his contacts with the outside world are maintained. Outside contacts are therefore encouraged especially between an inmate and his family and friends.'
5 In connection with his own research, Holt (1972) observed, 'The central finding of this research is the strong and consistent positive relationship that exists between parole success and maintaining strong family ties while in prison.'
6 Letter from prisoner, sent at the instigation of prison chaplain.
7 See Chapter 3 'The Problems of the Mother'.
8 Unless of course it is known that a probation officer is currently involved.
9 See Chapter 4, 'What are Children Told?'
10 Huxley-Robinson (1985).
11 Morris (1967). This short paper in the British Journal of Criminology is of great interest, even if some of the suggestions contained in it would be challenged today. Regretably, it is likely that only a few of the people directly concerned would have seen it; this is the consequence of its being published in an academic criminological journal.

12 Morris op.cit.
13 See Chapter 7.
14 Mrs Christine Graham, HALOW, 5 Onslow Road, Southampton, S02 0JD, Telephone Southampton 229359.
15 Hardwick (1986). Available direct from the publisher, Pepar Publications, 50 Knightlow Road, Birmingham B17 8QB, price £4.50, inclusive of post and packing.
16 This comment is not meant to imply that voluntary initiatives should be 'taken over' or 'bureaucratised'—far from it. However, facilities have no national coordination so that many potential recipients miss out as a result.
17 Morris op. cit.
18 Morris op. cit.
19 Personal correspondence.
20 Interview with teacher.
21 Interview with prisoner's wife.

APPENDIX

Policy Document of the Leicester Prison Visits Centre[1]

Statement of aims

The Visits Centre exists to provide a facility for the families, children and friends of men in prison. It offers, through its volunteer network, support, advice, friendship and practical assistance. Whilst recognising that some visitors may appropriately be referred to other agencies for specific help, all visitors will be encouraged to maintain links with the Centre during the period of the man's imprisonment.

In furtherance of these aims, the following objectives have been set:

(1) The Management Committee of the Centre has the overall responsibility for the operation of the Centre and for ensuring that the aims are met. The coordination of all the activities at the Centre will be undertaken by the Volunteer Coordinator. The Coordinator will be a member of the Management Committee, will attend it's meetings and will report to the Committee at these meetings.

(2) The Centre will be open from 10.30 am to 3.30 pm on Monday to Saturday each week. The Centre will be staffed during all opening periods by a rota of volunteers.

(3) Buses will be run on a regular basis to Ashwell, Ranby, Stafford and Featherstone Prisons, with a view to further development in this area.

(4) The needs of the children will be recognised by the provision of playgroup and crèche facilities.

(5) Opportunities will be provided for women to meet as a group as, and when, the need is identified.

(6) Every man received into Leicester Prison, who has family living within the Greater Leicester area, can expect a home visit from a volunteer within a few days of his reception.

(7) The Coordinator will ensure that the families of all imprisoned

men shall be made aware of the facilities at the Centre by means of a leaflet sent out from the prison on the man's reception.

(8) In order that all the above objectives can be met, regular fund-raising activities will need to take place.

(9) Work will be undertaken to extend and develop a pool of information on all matters relating to prison visiting both locally and nationally, and on DHSS entitlements concerning visits to prisons.

(10) It is a further objective of the Centre to increase public awareness of the needs of prisoner's families and to collect such data as is necessary to bring about a greater understanding of the consequences of imprisonment.

Note

1 Leicester Prison Visits Centre, 30 Tower Street, Leicester LE1 6WS; telephone 0533 544706.

References

Anderson, N., 1966. 'Prisoners' Families: A Study of Family Crisis'. Thesis on microfilm (University of Minnesota).

Arber, S. and Sawyer, L., 1985. 'The Role of the Receptionist in General Practice: A Dragon Behind the Desk?' *Soc. Sci. Med.* **20** 9, 911.

Bakker, L., Morris, B. and Janus, L., 1978. 'Hidden Victims of Crime', *Social Work*, March.

Baldwin, John and Bottoms, A.E., 1976. *The Urban Criminal*. London (Tavistock).

Bartle, R., 1986. 'Moral Problems of Punishment', *Justice of the Peace*, 15 November.

Box, Steven, 1986. 'Crime and Punishment', *Unemployment Unit Bulletin*, February.

Blackler, C., 1968. 'Primary Recidivism in Adult Men: Differences Between Men on First & Second Prison Sentence', *British Journal of Criminology* 8, 2, 130.

Blackwell, J., 1959. 'The Effects of Involuntary Separation on Selected Families of Men Committed to Prison from Spokane County, Washington'. Thesis (State College of Washington).

Braithwaite, J., 1981. 'The Myth of Social Class and Criminality Reconsidered', *American Sociological Review* 46, 36.

Brodsky, S., 1975. *Families and Friends of Men in Prison*. Lexington, USA (D.C. Heath).

Casale, S., 1984. *Minimum Standards for Prison Establishments*. London (NACRO).

Central Statistical Office, 1985. *Annual Abstract of Statistics*. London (HMSO).

Childright, 1985. 'Speaking for Children' leading article in *Childright* magazine 14, February 1985.

Clarke, Ruth, 1985. 'Two Heads Can be Better than One', *Social Work Today* 6 May.

Coker, J.B. and Martin, J.P., 1985. *Licensed to Live*. London (Blackwell).

Copley, C., 1981. 'Aspects of the Effects of the Penal Environment on Familial Relationships'. Thesis, London (Home Office; Prison Department).

de Crayencour, B., 1976. *Les Familles et Enfants de Detenus*. Brussels (International Catholic Child Bureau).

Davis, L., 1983. 'A Web of Punishment', *Social Work Today*, 14, 48, 21.

DHSS and Home Office, 1976. 'NAI to Children: the Police and Case Conferences', LASSL (76) 26 HC (76) 50 179/76.

DHSS, 1980. 'Child Abuse: Central Register Systems', LASSL (80) 4.

Drake, E.A., 1981. 'Helping Children Cope with Divorce: the Role of the School' in Stuart, I.R. and Abt, L.E., *Children of Separation and Divorce* (Van Nostran Rheinhold).

Dunn, Judy, 1984. *Sisters and Brothers*, London (Fontana).

Evans, Peter, 1986. 'Paying for Crime' in *The Times* 21 May.

Families Outside, 1984. *First Annual Report 1983/84*, 146 Holland Street, Glasgow, G2 4NG.

Farrington, D.P., 1981.'The Prevalence of Convictions'. *British Journal of Criminology*, 21, 2, 173.

Feaver, N., 1985. 'Beyond Control and Unruliness Among Juveniles'. Unpublished Cropwood Fellowship paper (Cambridge Institute of Criminology).

Fenton, N., 1959. *The Prisoner's Family: A study of Family Counseling in an Adult Correctional System*. Palo Alto (Pacific Books).

Forde, R.A., 1978. 'Twin Studies, Inheritance and Criminality', *British Journal of Criminology*, 18, 1.

Francis, P., Heygate, S., King, S. and Jones, M., 1983. 'Mightier Than The Sword', *Social Work Today*, 14, 17.

Francis, P. and Shaw, R.G., 1981. 'Divorce and the Law and Order Lobby', *Family Law*, 11, 3.

Freeman, M.D.A., 1983. *The Rights and Wrongs of Children*, London (Francis Pinter).

Friedman, S. and Esselstyn, T., 1965. 'The Adjustment of Children of Jail Inmates', *Federal Probation*, 29, 4.

Goffman, E., 1961. *Asylums*. New York (Anchor Books).

Hansard, 1985. Written answers, 9 July 1985.

Hardwick, Dave, 1986. *Serving the Second Sentence*. Birmingham (Pepar Publications).

HM Chief Inspector of Prisons, 1983. *Report on HM Prison, Parkhurst*. London (Home Office).

HM Chief Inspector of Prisons, 1984. *Prison Categorisation Procedures*. London (Home Office).

Hirschi, T. and Hindelang, M.J., 1977. 'Intelligence & Delinquency: A Revisionist Review', *American Sociological Review*, 42, 571.

Holt, N., 1972. 'Explorations in Inmate-Family Relationships', A Synopsis of *Research Report Number 46* (California Department of Corrections).

Home Office, 1978. Circular Instruction 45/1978.

Home Office, 1978. 'A Survey of the South East Prison Population', *Research Bulletin* 5, 12.

Home Office, 1979. *Committee of Inquiry into the United Kingdom Prison Services (May Report)*. London (HMSO).

Home Office, 1984. *Criminal Justice—a working paper*. London (HMSO). Also revised edition 1986.

Home Office, 1984. 'Intermittent Custody' Cmnd 9281. London (HMSO).

Home Office, 1985. *Prison Statistics England and Wales 1984*. London (HMSO).

Home Office, 1984. *Probation Service in England and Wales—Statement of National Objectives and Priorities*. London (Home Office).

Home Office, 1984. *Report on the Work of the Prison Department 1983*. London (HMSO).

Home Office, 1985. 'Criminal Careers of those Born in 1953, 1958 and 1963'. *Statistical Bulletin* 7, 1985.

Home Office, 1986. *Crime Prevention and the Community Programme*. London (Crime Prevention Unit).

Hope, Tim, 1986. 'Council Tenants and Crime', Home Office Research Bulletin 21, London.

Hough, M. and Mayhew, P., 1983. *The British Crime Survey: First Report*, Home Office Research Study No. 76. London (HMSO).

Hough, M. and Mayhew, P., 1985. *Taking Account of Crime: Key Findings from the 1984 British Crime Survey*, Home Office Research Study No. 85. London HMSO.

Hounslow, B., Stephenson, A., Stewart, J. and Crancher, J., 1982. *Children of Imprisoned Parents* (The Family and Children's Services Agency, Ministry of Youth and Community Services of New South Wales, Australia).

Howard League, 1979. *Losing Touch*. London (Howard League).

Howard League, 1985. *Unlawful Sex*, Report of a Howard League Working Party. London (Waterlow).

Huxley-Robinson, M., 1985. 'Counselling the Bereaved Child: The Role of the School Nurse', *Health Visitor*, September Vol. 58.

Jones, David N., 1982. *Understanding Child Abuse*. Sevenoaks (Hodder & Stoughton).

Justice, 1983. *Justice in Prison* London (Justice Educational and Research Trust). 'Justice' is the International Commission of Jurists.

Knight, C., 1984. *See* Leicester Prison Visits Centre Trust 1984 below.

Lea, J., Young, J., 1984. *What is to be done about Law and Order?* Harmondsworth (Penguin).

Leicester Prison Visits Centre Trust, 1984. Submission to House of Commons Home Affairs Committee on Remands in Custody.

Leicestershire Probation Service, 1979. 'Divorce Experience Course—A Guide for Staff Members', Leicester.

MacLennan, E., Fitz, J. and Sullivan, J., 1985. *Working Children*. London (Low Pay Unit).

Marsh, A., Dobbs, J. Monk, J. and White, A., 1985. *Staff Attitudes in the Prison Service*. London (HMSO).

Matthews, Jill, 1983. *Forgotten Victims*. London (NACRO).

Mathiesen, T., 1966. 'The Sociology of Prisons', *British Journal of Sociology*, 17, 1966.

Mednick, Sarnoff and Christiansen, Karl O., 1977. *Biosocial Bases of Criminal Behavior*. New York (Gardner Press Inc.).

Monger, Jill, 1970. 'Prisoner's Children' Dissertation for the Department of Social and Administrative Studies, University of Oxford.

Monger, M. and Pendleton, J., 1977. 'The Prison Visit', *Social Work Today*, 8, 34.

Monger, M. and Pendleton, J., 1981. 'Throughcare with Prisoners' Families', *Social Work Studies* Number 3, University of Nottingham.

Morris, Allison, 1978. *Juvenile Justice?* London (Heinemann).

Morris, Allison, Giller Henri, Szwed Elizabeth and Geach, Hugh, 1980. *Justice for Children*. London (Macmillan).

Morris, Pauline, 1965. *Prisoners & Their Families*, London (George Allen & Unwin).

Morris, Pauline, 1967. 'Fathers in Prison', *British Journal of Criminology* 7, 424.

NACRO, 1981. 'Fine Default', Report of a NACRO Working Party. London (NACRO).

NACRO, 1985. 'Home Leave', NACRO Briefing, July.

NACRO, 1985. 'The Use of Imprisonment—Some Facts and Figures', NACRO briefing, August 1985.

NACRO, 1985. 'Visits to Prisoners', NACRO Briefing, October.

NACRO, 1986. *Nacro Digest* Number 38 April.

NACRO, 1986. *News Digest* Number 39 June.

National Association of Probation Officers, 1981. *Social Inquiry Reports—A Policy Statement*. NAPO.

National Association of Senior Probation Officers, 1982. 'Probation Officers in Prison Department Establishments' Professional Committee Paper Number 2, *NASPO News* 4, 1982.

Ouston, Janet, 1984. 'Delinquency, Family Background & Educational Attainment', *British Journal of Criminology* 24, 1.

Page, Robert M., 1984. *Stigma*. London (Routledge & Kegan Paul).

Phillips, Kate, 1985. 'Into the Poverty Trap', *Nursing Mirror*, 160, 10, 18.

Priestley, P., 1980. *Community of Scapegoats*, Oxford (Pergamon Press).

Prison Department, 1983. *Prison Rules 1964* as amended by The Prison (Amendment) Rules of 1968, 1971, 1972, 1974, 1976, 1981, 1982 & 1983.

Prison Department, 1984. *Current Recommended Standards for the Design of New Prison Establishments*. London (Home Office).

Raynor, Lois, 1980. *The Adopted Child Comes of Age*, National Institute Social Services Library No. 36. London (George Allen & Unwin).

Report of the Control Review Committee, 1984. *Managing the Long Term Prison System*. London (HMSO).

Riley, David and Shaw, Margaret, 1985. *Parental Supervision and Juvenile Delinquency*, Home Office Research Study No. 83. London (HMSO).

Riley, Jeni and Lund, Mary, 1984. 'Schools Caught in the Middle' Paper delivered to 'Families Need Fathers' Day Conference, London, 22 November 1984.

Rourke, Myrna, 1984. 'Coping strategies of Mothers of Toddlers', *Nursing Times*, 16 May 1984.

Rowlands, Peter, 1980. *Saturday Parent*. London (George Allen & Unwin).

Rusche, G. and Kirchheimer, O., 1939. *Punishment and Social Structure*. New York (Columbia University Press).

Rutter, M., 1977. 'Parent Child Separation: Psychological Effects on Children', *Journal of Child Psychology and Psychiatry* 12, 233.

Schneller, D., 1978. *The Prisoner's Family*. San Francisco (R & E Research Associates).

Shaw, R.G., 1981. *Who Uses Social Inquiry Reports?* University of Cambridge (Institute of Criminology).

Shaw, R.G., 1982. 'The Myths of Prison Overcrowding', *NASPO News* 3, 1982.

Shaw, R.G., 1984. 'Shared Social Work in a Local Prison—A Matter of Trust', *Prison Service Journal* No. 55, July.

Shaw, R.G., 1986. 'Coal, Conviction and Calamity' *NASPO News* 6, 1.

Shaw, R.G., 1986. 'Kinderen van gedetineerden' in *De vrijheidsstraf* Eds. Jong, Neut & Tulkens Arnhem (Gouda Quint Bv). Book produced to commemorate 100 years of the Dutch Penal Code. (Paper by Shaw in English.)

Shaw, R.G., 1986. 'The Prevalence of Children of Imprisoned Fathers', *NASPO News* 6, 4.

Shaw, R.G., 'Schools and Prisoners' Children' forthcoming paper.

Shaw, R.G., 'Health Visitors and Prisoners' Children' forthcoming paper.

Shaw, R. and Hutchison, R. (eds), 1985. *Periodic Restriction of Liberty*. Cambridge (Institute of Criminology).

Shaw, S., 1982. 'The Peoples Justice' Prison Reform Trust Poll, *The Observer*, 21 March 1982.

Sparks, Richard F., 1971. *Local Prisons: The Crisis in the English Penal System*. London (Heinemann).

Speck, Peter, 1985. 'Counselling on Death and Dying', *British Journal of Guidance and Counselling* 13, 1.

Spicer, Faith, 1977. *Adolescence and Stress*. London (Forbes).

Vercoe, Kate, 1968. *Helping Prisoners' Families*. London (NACRO).

Wadsworth, M., 1979. *The Roots of Delinquency*. London (Martin Robertson).

Walker, Nigel, 1979. 'The Efficacy and Morality of Deterrents', *Criminal Law Review* 129.

Walker, N and Marsh, C., 1984. 'Do Sentences Affect Public Disapproval?', *British Journal of Criminology* 24, 1.

Wallerstein, Judith, 1984. Children of Divorce: Preliminary Report of a Ten Year Follow-up of Young Children', *American Journal of Orthopsychiatry* 54, 3.

West, D.J. and Farrington, D.P., 1973. *Who Becomes Delinquent?* London (Heinemann).

West, D.J., 1982. *Delinquency—Its Roots, Careers and Prospects*. London (Heinemann).

West Glamorgan Probation Service, 1979. 'A Project Looking at the Problems of Prisoners' Families in Swansea'.

Willcox, P., 1981. 'Why Are They Here?', *NASPO News* 2, 81.

Willcox, P., 1983. 'How Valid Was Why Are They Here?', *NASPO News* 2, 83.

Williams, J., 1968. *Conditions for Visitors to Prisons*. London (Prison Department, Home Office).

Williams, J., 1978. *Conditions for Visitors to Prisons—A Reassessment*. London (Prison Department, Home Office).

Williams, Pauline, 1984. 'Innocent Until Proved Guilty', *Criminal Justice* 2, 1.

Wilmer, *et al*, 'Group Treatment of Prisoners and their Families', *Mental Hygiene* 50, 380. Quoted by Monger & Pendleton (1981).

Wilson, G., 1984. 'I know while he is in prison he's safe', *New Society* 1 November.

Wilson, H., 1974. 'Parenting in Poverty', *British Journal of Social Work* 4, 241.

Wilson, H., 1982. 'Parental Responsibility and Delinquency: Reflections on a White Paper Proposal', *Howard Journal* 21, 1, 23.

Wilson, H., 1983. 'Family Influences on Juvenile Misbehaviour', *Health Visitor* 56, 376 October.

Wilson, H., 1985. Paper delivered to the British Society of Criminology in London on 22 May 1985 and summarised in the Newsletter of the Society 3, 1985.

Wilson, H. and Herbert, G.W., 1978. *Parents and Children in the Inner City.* London (Routledge & Kegan Paul).

Wright, J.F., 1984. Letter in *Criminal Justice* 2, 2.

Index